UN
CENSO
RED
TRUTH

"Jud Wilhite is one of the youngest pastors of America's largest and fastest growing churches and has introduced thousands of people to Jesus .... Out of biblical conviction and pastoral affection he has written this readable and helpful book on core Christian conviction that will benefit Christians and non-Christians alike."

—**MARK DRISCOLL,** Founding Pastor of Mars Hill Church;
author, *Vintage Jesus*

"John Wesley prayed that God would light him on fire so that others could watch him burn. Reading this book you get the sense of a man on fire. Fresh, doctrinally sound, historic Christianity immersed in passion and aflame in the Holy Spirit, communicated with humor by one of America's brightest young pastors—I am very excited about this book!"

—**J. D. GREEAR,** Lead Pastor of Summit Church;
author, *Breaking the Islam Code*

"Jud Wilhite is a fresh voice for leadership and authenticity. He's on the cutting edge of reaching people, through a dynamic church that is making a difference around the world. He has high integrity and I admire him like crazy for what he's doing to bring clarity to people about who Christ is for their life."

—**DINO RIZZO,** Lead Pastor of Healing Place Church;
author, *Servolution*

"Jud has a gift for making biblical truth accessible to people who might otherwise feel intimidated by the Bible. He's right there with the reader—never placing himself above anyone else. I recommend this book to explain the faith to anyone who wants to hear."

—**SARAH SUMNER**, Dean of A.W. Tozer Theological Seminary;
author, *Leadership Above the Line*

// JUD WILHITE

UN CENSO RED

TRUTH

A NO-SPIN GUIDE TO THE CHRISTIAN FAITH

ethur

UNCENSORED TRUTH

Distributed by Ethur
P. O. Box 77862
Corona, CA 92877

ISBN 978-1-888741-27-8

Printed in the United States of America
2010—First Edition
10 9 8 7 6 5 4 3 2 1

to Mary Wilhite
1929-2009

FORE
WORD//

✳ ✳ ✳ One of the most inaccurate yet persistent miscon-ceptions about large, growing churches is that their growth is somehow caused by offering a *watered down* message. Those who perpetuate this myth are actually revealing their fundamen-tal lack of faith in the power of the Bible as God's Word. They don't believe the Word has the ability to attract large crowds without being compromised. They assume that large churches couldn't possibly attract that many people if they preached the pure, unadulterated Word of God. This presumption—that all large churches automatically compromise the truth to make it more palatable and that all small churches are automatically more faithful to the Word—is, in a word, pure baloney! It is a myth based more on envy and jealousy than on reality.

The truth is that when God's Word is preached clearly, compellingly, and completely, it attracts people! If this wasn't true, how do you explain the multitudes and huge crowds that swarmed to hear Jesus teach? Jesus certainly didn't compromise his message to attract a crowd, yet the Bible says, "Enormous crowds followed him wherever he went,"[1] and "the large crowd listened to him with delight."[2] No one accused Jesus of watering down the message except the jealous chief priests who resented his popularity. We must remember that their motive for crucify-ing Jesus was envy.[3]

One of the obvious characteristics of Jesus' ministry was that it attracted crowds. *Large* crowds. *Enormous* crowds. Multi-tudes. Genuine Christ-like teaching does the same thing today.

---

1   *Matthew 4:25*, TLB.

2   *Mark 12:37*, TLB.

3   *Mark 15:12.*

Preaching like Jesus has a magnetic quality about it. You don't have to use gimmicks or compromise your convictions to gather a crowd. You just have to teach the way Jesus did. That's what this book by my dear friend and partner in ministry is all about. Jud Wilhite is Exhibit A of how God's Word, taught simply and lovingly, attracts and transforms lives.

In *Uncensored Truth,* Jud demonstrates that vibrant Christians and churches can be built on an uncompromised commitment to God's Word and the application of its truth in ways that transform. The truth sets us free. If we genuinely obey the Word, not just debate or defend it, we can't help but grow in spiritual maturity.

As a pastor, I've noticed that many Christians think that true spiritual maturity is so far out of their reach they don't even attempt to attain it. We must continually remind them that spiritual maturity is not just for so-called *super-saints.* It is God's desired goal for every one of his children.

Paul often compared the Christian life to athletics, reminding us that we must train ourselves in order to stay in top spiritual shape. In many ways, the path to spiritual fitness parallels the path to becoming physically fit. In both cases, it is a matter of developing healthy habits and being disciplined enough to stick with them.

Uncensored Truth will help you develop the perspective, the convictions, the habits, and the skills you need for spiritual maturity. Get ready to grow!

—Rick Warren
Founding Pastor of Saddleback Church;
bestselling author, *The Purpose Driven Life*

VIBRANT CHRISTIANS AND
CHURCHES CAN BE BUILT
ON AN UNCOMPROMISED
COMMITMENT TO
GOD'S WORD AND THE
APPLICATION OF ITS TRUTH
IN WAYS THAT TRANSFORM!

INTRO
DUC
TION //

✳ ✱ ✳ I am a sucker for uncensored grace: the radical, amazing, overwhelming favor and forgiveness of God given to undeserving people like myself. Christians and churches have too often tried to domesticate grace. We love to tame it. We appreciate it, talk about it, and even try to market it. We believe in grace, but not enough to do any serious damage to the walls that separate us from others. But when your eyes have been opened, as mine have been, to see thousands of people the religious world has considered too far gone actually experience transformation through faith in Jesus, you can't help but be forever marked.

I am.

God's grace is beyond my small-minded boundaries and categories. His love for people lost in the darkest darkness consistently amazes me. His mercy for those who deserve it least, like me, is astounding.

I've written about the wonders of grace in a previous book titled *Uncensored Grace: Stories of Hope from the Streets of Las Vegas.* Uncensored grace lives in church communities where CEOs, soccer moms, strippers, doctors, dealers, and everyone in between can arrive at a place of belief and eventually become all God would have them be. Churches that thrive on uncensored grace acknowledge that we're all sinners in need of grace, so they accept people where they are and maintain that it's okay to not be okay. Because, in fact, none of us are okay in and of ourselves.

Real grace banks on this unvarnished truth about ourselves; it constitutes the ultimate honesty about the condition of our hearts. In fact, without this brutal honesty, this uncensored truth, grace would be much less amazing (or no grace at all). Grace and truth form two sides of the same coin. You can't have one without the other. John wrote of Jesus: "We have seen his glory, glory as of the only Son from the Father, full of *grace* and *truth*.... And from his fullness we have all received, grace upon grace. For the law was given through Moses; *grace* and *truth* came through Jesus Christ."[1]

Jesus embodied both grace and truth perfectly. As his followers, we must seek to embody them as well.

Grace exists because of the uncensored truths of the sovereign God who saved us through the life, death, and resurrection of Jesus. Grace takes root in our hearts through the indwelling power of the Holy Spirit. Grace comes alive in all its beauty through the truth of God's Word. Any alleged grace without these truths amounts to little more than self-help and truncated faith. We are left with what Richard Niebuhr called "a God without wrath who brought men without sin into a kingdom without judgment through the ministrations of a Christ without a cross."[2]

The temptation we face is to censor the harsh realities of sin, judgment, and the cross. Doing so certainly makes God more popular, but it also makes his ways and means frustratingly ambiguous. For instance, on one of my favorite TV shows—*24*—I watched a Muslim cleric walk into the hospital room where hero Jack Bauer (played by Kiefer Sutherland) lies on his deathbed, confessing the horrible things he's done. Jack fears he won't have time to right his wrongs and make amends. But the cleric assures him that he still has time to make everything right. Then he prays this prayer for Jack: "Let us all forgive ourselves for all the wrong we have done."

What a nice little prayer. Nice . . . and totally lame.

I watched this, and I was thinking, *What?!*

The Hollywood angle on faith and forgiveness is revealing in its utter vacuity. It's easy and lightweight, unworthy of the "horrible things" it means to address. There's simply nothing to it.

Although I'm a big fan of Jack Bauer, I know he does not

---

1   *John 1:14, 16-17, ESV, emphasis added.*

2   *H. Richard Niebuhr, The Kingdom of God in America (New York: Harper & Row, 1959), 193.*

have the power or authority to give forgiveness to himself. That's one action maneuver he's not going to be capable of. Jack does need forgiveness, and he needs it *from* somebody. He needs it from God. But in this scene there is no conversation about God or faith or eternity or Jesus or Muhammad or their differences. Nope, nothing but a lame self-help message for a guy who has pulled out people's fingernails, slit throats, and performed electric shock on terrorists with the cord from a table lamp. Jack definitely needs more than trite self-forgiveness. (At the very least he could stand a little "How's that working for ya?" confrontation from the government's best version of Dr. Phil or something.)

I know it's only TV, and there's still hope for Jack Bauer as long as there is a next season, but we ourselves run the risk of dumbing down our faith to the point of empty clichés. The core truths of the Christian faith are vitally important, and the desperate need of our day is to talk about them, to wrestle with them, and to live them out. We need both uncensored grace and uncensored truth.

It is in vogue among some Christian leaders today to shy away from any truth claims. They feel that claims of certainty about some or all foundational beliefs can erect boundary lines that mark people as "in" or "out" based on beliefs. They resist clarity, preferring "mystery." They talk about engaging in a "spiritual journey" (as do I), but some of them seem to have no destination in mind. Many question whether we can really know anything true about God at all.

I would agree that we can't know everything about God, but didn't he communicate to us through thousands of pages in the Bible so we could know *some* things? Some important, necessary things? Part of uncensoring truth is accepting that truth claims challenge and define us.

Others deny that Jesus came to save us from our sins, saying instead that he primarily came to show us a better way to live. Jesus as "good example" is just warmed-over feel-good religion. I definitely believe Jesus shows us a better way to live, but isn't our ability to imitate Jesus made possible only because he came to die in our place on the cross? We're saved *for* good works, not by them.[3]

All of this is to say, I've grown weary of the ambiguity toward Jesus and the animosity toward the church that some champion. I'm a follower of Jesus who seeks to align my beliefs with historic Christianity. God in his amazing grace saved me and used a church community to help me heal and grow. I'm not just the pastor of a church; I'm a product of the church. I love the church and want to see it thrive in the grace and truth of Jesus.

Where I live, in the Las Vegas area, Christian church attendance is at one of the lowest rates in the nation. Many do not define themselves as Christian. Yet even among those who do, they often can't tell you much of what being a Christian means. They are unclear or confused about what the Bible says about everything from who God is to the return of Jesus to heaven and hell. There is a desperate need among believers to understand what the Christian faith is all about.

My goal in *Uncensored Truth* is to clarify and commend the beliefs that constitute historic Christianity. We'll explore what the Bible says about God, Jesus, the Holy Spirit, salvation, the church, angels and demons, the return of Jesus, and heaven and hell. I would not consider all of the beliefs that I describe in this book as essentials to being a Christian, but I do believe that many of them are, and they are all important enough to wrestle through.

A final word to those always looking for a new, creative, fresh take on Christianity:

I recall a particular journalist who visited our church for a story he was writing. He talked first of his excitement as he walked in. He dug the loud music, the young vibe, the pastor who dressed like a "roadie for Nickelback." He hoped for a new version of Christianity, and he thought he'd found it. But the longer I talked during the message time, the more frustrated he became.

---

3 *Ephesians 2:10; Galatians 5:1.*

He eventually ended his article by saying with annoyance that if you wanted to know Jud Wilhite's perspective, "see the Bible." This was the greatest backhanded compliment he could have given me.

I honestly pray that there's nothing here that isn't represented in historic, orthodox Christianity.[4] But I would argue that these solid, historic truths are endlessly fresh and relevant. They come from the living God and therefore are creative and profound and insightful and glorious and liberating. These truths have pushed me to wonder, driven me to my knees, and spurred me to worship. They shape the heart of my relationship with God, and as I grow in them, I grow in my relationship with God. I believe that as you study them, you too will "grow in the grace and knowledge of our Lord and Savior Jesus Christ. All glory to him, both now and forever! Amen."[5]

---

4   The word orthodox comes from two Greek words. Ortho means "correct" or "right," and doxa means "belief." So when we speak of orthodox Christianity, we mean Christianity that is in keeping with what Christians have historically stated is "right belief."

5   2 Peter 3:18.

GOD IN
THE
FRAY//

✳ ✸ ✳ **Every one of us carry a picture of God in our hearts.** This picture comes primarily from what we heard about God in our childhood, but it also comes from the way we've seen him portrayed in movies or in books. For years, I pictured God as a cop just waiting to nail me with a radar gun. (This probably had something to do with the fact that I was living lawlessly and always looking over my shoulder for the real cops!) Later, after I became a believer, I saw him as an unmoved and unappeasable judge. All my efforts at good behavior did not give me much confidence about my standing with him.

Some see him as an angry God with a hair-trigger temper, punishing us with lightning bolts and hurricanes. Others see him as an old man with long white hair, benevolent but boring like Father Time. He's been pictured as the Guy in the Sky, the Man Upstairs, or even a cosmic Sugar Daddy. But who is he really?

Here's why these pictures matter: Your view of God will impact every area of your life. Your view of God will impact your view of people, of problems, of money, of work, of this life and the next. It will affect how you deal with challenges, how you handle pressure, and what you do with your time. It will affect your self-image and your self-esteem and of course your relationship with God and your relationships with others.

If you see God as a stern taskmaster, you will be reluctant to seek out his presence in times of guilt and shame, because you won't expect mercy from him. If you see God as a jolly but benign Santa Claus type, you may pray to him for good feelings and wishes, but you will probably find it hard to cling to him in times of extreme trouble and grief. If your God is the copilot god of the now-clichéd "Footprints" poem, you may think to turn to him when you're in trouble, but you won't be inclined to trust him as sovereign over your everyday life.

A believer whose view of God is hazy will live a confused Christian life. To put it bluntly, anyone whose picture of God is weak will live out a weak faith.

So where do we rehab our view of God? Where do we go to see the truest picture of God? We go to the Bible, where God gives us his own view of himself.

In the Beginning //

Witness how the Bible begins God's story: "In the beginning God created the heavens and the earth. The earth was formless and empty, and darkness covered the deep waters. And the Spirit of God was hovering over the surface of the waters. Then God said, 'Let there be light,' and there was light."[1]

Our God is a git'r done God. He's got a lifetime supply of Insta-Creation in his pinky finger. And as the curtains come back on the opening of Genesis, we see the ease of God's infinite power in stunning literary Technicolor. These first three verses of the Bible give us a glimpse into the unique quality of God that differentiates him from any other god. Verse one shows us God the authoritative Creator, God the Father. In the next sentence we see the Spirit hovering over the water, God's protective presence in creation. The following sentence reveals the Word of God as he speaks creation into being. In the Gospel of John, Jesus is described as the Word of God who became flesh and dwelt among us.[2] So the opening verses of the Bible contain references to the Father, the Son, and the Spirit—the Three-in-One.

Reading further in Genesis, we see God say, "Let *us* make human beings in *our* image."[3] In the story, no one has been created yet. So who is God talking to? Who is "us?" In this short

---

1   *Genesis 1:1-3.*
2   *John 1:1, 14.*
3   *Genesis 1:26, emphasis added.*

sentence we see the staggering truth that God is a community within himself!

The first picture the Bible gives of God's nature, then, is a snapshot of the fullness of his being: his triune nature. Clear enough so far? Well, put your seatbelt on, because we're about to speed over some amazing terrain. These verses lead us to the important concept of the Trinity.

> YOUR VIEW OF GOD WILL IMPACT
> EVERY AREA OF YOUR LIFE.
> YOUR VIEW OF PEOPLE,
> OF PROBLEMS, OF MONEY,
> OF WORK, OF THIS LIFE
> AND THE NEXT. //

Trinity: Not the Character in *The Matrix* //
Unfortunately, the only Trinity that most in our generation know is a character from *The Matrix*. But the real Trinity doesn't wear skintight leather and is infinitely more kick-tail. The real Trinity is our God, who exists in three persons.

Now, the term Trinity itself never actually appears in the Bible, though the concepts that led to the term are found in both the Old and New Testaments. (We'll get to the biblical evidence for the Trinity shortly.) The term actually first appeared in the early church, and it did so because people began to teach whacked-out things about God, Jesus, and the Holy Spirit. The church's nerds (who I respect deeply)—people like Justin Martyr, Ignatius, and Polycarp in the second century and Athanasius, Basil the Great, and Gregory of Nazianzus in the fourth century—started to talk about and defend the Trinity. They affirmed that there is one God, that Jesus is fully God and fully man, and that the Holy Spirit is God. They defended the Trinity, not to take away the mystery of who God is, but rather to ensure that the mystery remains. Defending the Trinity was essentially putting the smackdown on false teachers.

A BELIEVER WHOSE
VIEW OF GOD IS HAZY
WILL LIVE A CONFUSED
CHRISTIAN LIFE. TO PUT
IT BLUNTLY, ANYONE
WHOSE PICTURE OF GOD
IS WEAK WILL LIVE OUT
A WEAK FAITH.

The bottom line is this: people didn't make this stuff up. The idea that there is one God in three persons is found in Scripture and was believed—and later fought for—by the earliest Christians. I don't completely understand this mystery, and neither have Christian thinkers through the ages, but I do believe it is clearly represented in the text of the Bible.

God the Father //

The Father is the first person of the Trinity. He has all things under control. From the full context of the biblical story, we know that the Father is loving and good. He desires to save humanity and have a relationship with people, but he is also holy and just and will bring judgment upon sin.

Jesus spoke often about the Father. He taught us to pray by saying, "Our Father in heaven." He told us that the Father knows our needs and will provide for us. He called us to do the will of the Father.[4]

In fact, Jesus called God "Abba" when he prayed, as in the Garden of Gethsemane before his betrayal and crucifixion.[5] *Abba* is the Aramaic term for "Dad." It is the same term young Jewish kids would call their fathers. Jesus was the first person we know of to address God as "Dad," with this term of affection and care. This was unprecedented in the Jewish faith and in all the world religions.[6] Jesus reminds us that the awesome and powerful Creator is the compassionate and loving Father. Paul would later encourage us to run to his arms and exclaim, "Daddy," when he wrote, "Because we are his children, God has sent the Spirit of his Son into our hearts, prompting us to call out, 'Abba, Father.' "[7] And our Father doesn't even care if we have Kool-Aid mustaches or snot running out of our nose. He hugs us joyfully anyway.

---

4   *Matthew 6:8-9; 12:50.*

5   *Mark 14:36.*

6   *See Robert H. Stein,* The Method and Message of Jesus' Teaching *(Louisville, KY: Westminster John Knox, 1994), 83–86.*

7   *Galatians 4:6.*

God the Son //

The second person of the Trinity is the Son, Jesus Christ. The Son is fully man and fully God. Jesus said, "The Father and I are one," and the crowd picked up stones to kill him because they knew he was claiming to be God. There will be more on the divinity of Jesus in a later chapter, but for the time being, we can see that Paul assumed from Jesus' words and works that Jesus was God incarnate. Paul wrote that Jesus "was God" and "Christ is the visible image of the invisible God." John told us that Jesus was present at the beginning, and Jesus himself told us, "Before Abraham was even born, I Am!"[8] (By the way, there is no comeback for this. "Before Abraham was even born, I Am!" is the trump card for all accusations and verbal assaults. Do not try it at home, however; Jesus is a trained professional.)

Historic Christian faith clearly teaches that Jesus the Son of God is equal to and eternal with God the Father.

God the Spirit //

The third person of the Trinity is the Holy Spirit. The Bible is full of references to the Spirit and his work to comfort, instruct, and correct believers. Throughout Paul's letters in the New Testament, he consistently referred to the Holy Spirit as "the Spirit of God" and "God's Spirit," reminding us constantly to afford the Spirit the same reverence we would God the Father. And in other places, his language reminds us that the Spirit works in concert with the Father and the Son.[9] (A later chapter will detail more fully the teaching of the Holy Spirit.)

Tri-unity //

We see the Trinity popping up in several places throughout the Bible. Consider this example: "After his baptism, as *Jesus* came

---

8 *John 10:30, 33; Philippians 2:6; Colossians 1:15; John 1:1; 8:58.*

9 *"May the grace of the Lord Jesus Christ, the love of God, and the fellowship of the Holy Spirit be with you all"* *(2 Corinthians 13:14). "Because we are his children, God has sent the Spirit of his Son into our hearts, prompting us to call out, 'Abba, Father' " (Galatians 4:6).*

up out of the water, the heavens were opened and he saw the *Spirit of God* descending like a dove and settling on him. And a *voice from heaven* said, 'This is my dearly loved Son, who brings me great joy.' "[10] Jesus is in the water. The Spirit descends like a dove. The Father speaks from heaven. In this snapshot we see our one God present in his three persons.

Want some more examples? We also see a reference to the Trinity in Jesus' final commission to his followers. He commanded us to "go and make disciples of all the nations, baptizing them in the name of the *Father* and the *Son* and the *Holy Spirit*." And then Paul said, "May the grace of the *Lord Jesus Christ*, the love of *God*, and the fellowship of the *Holy Spirit* be with you all."[11]

Our amazing God is a triune God.

One of the cool things we learn from the Trinity is the value of community. God in his very being is a community of three persons loving each other perfectly. This is why God values relationships and why we should value them as well. God's design for us doesn't come just from his good ideas but also from his great nature.

Our relationships and communities ought to be patterned on the love, sacrifice, and authority demonstrated in the community of God himself. Just as the Trinity exemplifies a beautiful dance of love and mutual submission among the Father, Son and Holy Spirit, so the Christian community is meant to revel in kindness toward one another, showing grace at every turn. It's a beautiful dance of our own, one that shines brightly like an uncovered lamp in the darkness or a landmark city on a hill.[12] God exists in community and invites us to share communion with him and with one another.

THE REAL TRINITY DOESN'T WEAR SKINTIGHT LEATHER AND IS INFINITELY MORE KICK-TAIL. THE REAL TRINITY IS OUR GOD, WHO EXISTS IN THREE PERSONS. //

---

10 *Matthew 3:16-17, emphasis added.*

11 *Matthew 28:19, emphasis added; 2 Corinthians 13:14, emphasis added.*

12 *Matthew 5:14-15.*

What Makes God *God*? //

Now that we've explored God's triune nature (granted, from a view of fifty thousand feet), let's check out God's character. God's attributes are the qualities that make God *God*! Since God is bigger than anything we can understand, it is impossible to explain everything about him or to break him down into bite-size pieces. We are like ants trying to understand and explain a jumbo jet. But it is still helpful to organize what we do know based on what the Bible teaches about God.

1. God is eternal and self-existent. God exists eternally apart from all creation. He is self-sufficient and has no need for anything or anyone. Before you were or anything else was, God existed. He has always been and he always will be.

When Moses asked God what his name was, God replied, "I Am Who I Am."[13] In Moses' time and culture, people worshiped the sun god, the god of fertility, the god of the harvest, the god of rain, the god of nacho cheese, and so on. So as God gave Moses a message to deliver, he naturally wondered, "Whom shall I say is speaking? Which God are you?" God said, "I Am." This phrase comes from the verb "to be" and could read, "I Will Be Who I Will Be." (If I were Moses, I'd be like, "Thanks a lot, God. Like that really clears it up!") It is almost as if God is saying, "Look, Mo, if you think you can define me or understand everything about me, you can't. I'm mysterious, amazing, and incredible. I will be who I will be. I am who I am."

But God is not Popeye ("I yam who I yam"). He's not apologizing for *how* he is; he is declaring *who* he is. "I Am" clues us in to God's eternal and infinite personhood. He always was, always is, and always will be.

You and I are temporal. We've all been sucking up oxygen for a relatively short time, and we have plenty of needs. But God Almighty needs nothing and relies on nothing. He is eternally self-supporting. He is more majestic than we can ever comprehend.

---

13 *Exodus 3:13-14.*

He has no limits or boundaries except for those that would violate his character. (For instance, God can't be evil.) There is no one like him. He is sufficient in himself. He is above all and in all and over all. He is God!

Years ago I heard Louie Giglio speak on the name of God. His message reduced me to tears, and the truth of what he said convicted me to the core. I had put myself at the center of my universe, but as Louie put it:

> God was telling Moses: I AM the center of everything. I AM running the show. I AM the same every day, forever. I AM the owner of everything. I AM the Lord. I AM the Creator and Sustainer of life. I AM the Savior. I AM more than enough. I AM inexhaustible and immeasurable. I AM God. . . . In a heartbeat, Moses knew God's name—and something more. He finally knew his. If God's name is I AM, Moses' name must be I am not. *I am not* the center of everything. *I am not* in control. *I am not* the solution. *I am not* all-powerful. *I am not* calling the shots. *I am not* the owner of anything. *I am not* the Lord.[14]

It may be an odd exercise to define ourselves according to what we are not, but we learn from the Bible that we're supposed to decrease and God is supposed to increase.[15] The first half of the gospel is acknowledging, "I am not worthy." But the great news is that God offers this response to our fallenness: "I AM salvation!" What a privilege we have to know this eternal God!

The Bible says that, to the Lord, a day is like a thousand years and a thousand years are like a day. (In our world, we call that phenomenon the DMV.) God is called "the eternal God."[16] Elsewhere we learn that his love is eternal, his laws are eternal, his word is eternal, and he is due eternal praise. Are you sensing a

---

14 Louie Giglio, I Am Not But I Know I AM *(Sisters, OR: Multnomah, 2005), 38-39.*

15 *John 3:30.*

16 *2 Peter 3:8; Genesis 21:33; Deuteronomy 33:27.*

pattern? God is eternal. There never was a time when he was not, and there never will be a time when he is not.

YOU AND I ARE TEMPORAL.
WE'VE ALL BEEN SUCKING UP OXYGEN
FOR A RELATIVELY SHORT TIME,
AND WE HAVE PLENTY OF NEEDS.
BUT GOD ALMIGHTY NEEDS NOTHING
AND RELIES ON NOTHING. //

2. God is all powerful. The theological term used for this characteristic is *omnipotent. Omni* means "all," and *potent* means "strong." God is all strong or almighty. He asks, "Behold, I am the LORD, the God of all flesh; is anything too difficult for Me?"[17]

This really isn't a question. It's like when your wife asks, "Do I look fat in these jeans?" Both questions are theoretical and hypothetical, but the wrong answer to either brings a world of pain. Is anything too difficult for God? The answer is an unequivocal no.

Think for a moment about God's power. He has power over creation. He brought the world into being with his voice and humankind into being with his breath. He has power over death and the grave and hell and Satan. He has the power to save a soul for eternity and he has power for you!

3. God is present everywhere. This attribute is called *omnipresence,* or all presence. God is everywhere in the universe at the same moment. He is present and aware of everything in creation. The psalmist declared in Psalm 139:7-10:

> *I can never escape from your Spirit!*
> > *I can never get away from your presence!*
> *If I go up to heaven, you are there;*
> > *if I go down to the grave, you are there.*

If I ride the wings of the morning,
if I dwell by the farthest oceans,
even there your hand will guide me,
and your strength will support me.

Where can we go to get away from the Spirit of God? Nowhere! There is no place on earth or in the heavens where a person can escape the watchful eye of God. God is not an absentee landlord. He is not out there in heavenly isolation, floating in the cosmos. He is not busy with something more important. He is by you and with you at this very moment. He is interested in you, watching over you, caring for you, available to you.

This can (and should) be cause for hope. The scholar Wayne Grudem reminds us that in the overwhelming number of times when the Bible refers to God's presence, that presence is to bless. He is everywhere and his desire is to bless us, his children. Grudem writes:

> It is in this way that we should understand God's presence above the ark of the covenant in the Old Testament. We read of "the ark of the covenant of the LORD of hosts, who is *enthroned on the cherubim*" (1 Sam. 4:4; cf. Ex. 25:22), a reference to the fact that God made his presence known and acted in a special way to bring blessing and protection to his people at the location he had designated as his throne, namely, the place above the two golden figures of heavenly beings ("cherubim") that were over the top of the ark of the covenant. It is not that God was not present elsewhere, but rather that here he especially made his presence known and here he especially manifested his character and brought blessing to his people.[18]

So the special presence of God, even when figuratively localized over an object that was carried into battle and could kill a

---

man who touched it, was meant overwhelmingly to be a blessing to God's people.

When the Bible talks of God being far away from the rebellious, it doesn't mean he is not there. God is present, but he is not present to bless the person whose heart has not turned to him.

Meanwhile, believers can take hope in the realization that there is no dark night we can go through that does not include him. There is no valley or mountain we face alone. He is always there!

4. God knows everything. He is *omniscient*, meaning all knowing. God knows himself and all of his creation, and he knows it all exhaustively. He knows everything immediately, simultaneously, and truly. He knows all the possible choices we may make *and* he knows ahead of time which one we *will* make. Because God is God, he is infinitely intelligent.

Paul worshiped God for his intelligence when he exclaimed, "Oh, how great are God's riches and wisdom and knowledge! How impossible it is for us to understand his decisions and his ways!"[19] The greatness and limitlessness of God's knowledge blew Paul's mind.

Just think about this: our bodies contain one hundred trillion cells with coiled strands of DNA that could stretch out to six feet long. That DNA has a chemical alphabet that provides the exact assembly instructions for the proteins in our bodies. Citing geneticist Michael Denton, Lee Strobel writes, "The information needed to build the proteins for all the species of organisms that have ever lived . . . 'could be held in a teaspoon and there would still be room left for all the information in every book ever written.' "[20] That is one teaspoon of pure DNA. God's mind is greater than an ocean of DNA. His wisdom is astounding. He knows everything.

---

19 *Romans 11:33.*
20 *Lee Strobel,* The Case for a Creator *(Grand Rapids, MI: Zondervan, 2004), 220.*

GOD IS FULLY AWARE
OF WHAT IS HAPPENING
AND WILL IN THE CORRECT TIME
BRING AN END TO THE CONFUSION
AND DISORDER IN HIS CREATION. //

There are some, however, who continue to challenge the notion of God's omniscience. For instance, a new push toward "open theism"—a general belief that denies God's exhaustive future foreknowledge—continues among professing Christians. One open theist writes, "God confronts a future that is open. The distinction between what is possible and what is actual is valid for God as well as for us. The past is actual, the present is becoming, and the future is possible." And later: "It would be a serious limitation if God could not experience surprise and delight."[21] But not as serious a limitation as, oh, I don't know, God not knowing the future.

The problems with open theism are several.[22]

First of all, insisting that God cannot know the future because it is yet to occur is a logical conclusion based on human limitations, not divine possibilities. Yes, we cannot know the future, because we live inside of time. But God does not. So for open theists to hold that God is in the dark about the future as we are is really a way of casting God in our own image.

Furthermore, the Bible says plenty about God knowing the future exhaustively, including knowing the future choices of his creatures. Jesus knew Peter was going to betray him, right down to the exact number of times. God says he makes known

21 Clark H. Pinnock, "Systematic Theology," in The Openness of God: A Biblical Challenge to the Traditional Understanding of God, eds. Clark H. Pinnock, Richard Rice, John Sanders, William Hasker, and David Basinger (Downers Grove, IL: InterVarsity Press, 1994), 120, 123.

22 Two good books engaging the challenge of open theism are Bruce A. Ware, God's Lesser Glory: The Diminished God of Open Theism (Wheaton, IL: Crossway, 2000); and John Piper, Justin Taylor, and Paul Kjoss Helseth, eds., Beyond the Bounds: Open Theism and the Undermining of Biblical Christianity (Wheaton, IL: Crossway, 2003).

the end from the beginning, which wouldn't be possible if he didn't know the end at the beginning.[23]

Open theism essentially makes God a really good guesser. But in the grand context of the Bible, we do not encounter a God subject to time and to the surprise acts of his creatures. Instead we encounter the awe-inspiring God of the universe, who is the Alpha and the Omega (beginning and end), who plans the course of humanity, who dictates prophecy, and who even knows how many hairs are on your head and what you'll have for breakfast tomorrow morning. You cannot catch God off guard; otherwise, he would not be God.

5. God is in control. There are plenty of times in life when we feel like things are out of control. We may experience financial troubles, physical ailments, or relational struggles. Hearing the words "I want a divorce," "It's cancer," or "You're fired" can send us into a tailspin. We could easily conclude that God is no longer in control of things and that therefore we have no one to trust and no place to get our bearings. But just the opposite is true. Even when the newspaper reports natural disasters, criminal acts, and economic downfalls, God is still in control. One of the great promises of Scripture is found in Romans 8:28: "God causes everything to work together for the good of those who love God and are called according to his purpose for them."

We live in a fallen world where sin and Satan complicate and destroy. Yet God is fully aware of what is happening and will in the correct time bring an end to the confusion and disorder in his creation. He doesn't say that everything that happens is good, but he does say that we can trust him for the redemption of even the worst of tragedies. Notice that Romans 8:28 says God "causes" everything to work together for the good. He is not passive, nor is he reactive. He is in control, ultimately, even of the hardships we face, even of the evil done to us. When

---

23 *Isaiah 46:10.*

THE BOTTOM LINE
IS THAT ALL THESE
CHARACTERISTICS OF GOD
SHOW BOTH HOW WHOLLY
OTHER GOD IS FROM US
AND HOW WHOLLY
FOR US HE CAN BE.

Joseph faced his brothers at the end of a long road of murderous intentions and bitter betrayal, when he had the perfect opportunity to open up a can on them (and not a can of diet soda), he instead said to them, "You meant evil against me, but God meant it for good."[24]

What all this means is that God is sovereign. He is the King and he is in control. Even sin and evil, which our holy God does not do himself, is nevertheless done under his sovereign allowance. The permission granted to the devil to tempt Job is an example of this.[25]

The bottom line is that all these characteristics of God show both how wholly *other* God is from us and how wholly *for us* he can be. Suppose God was not all knowing, all present, all powerful, and all sovereign. How confident would you be, then, that he could help you with the most difficult crises of your life, much less that he could actually save you from eternal death? These qualities give us confidence that God will protect us and see us through all of life's pitfalls.

What God Shares of Himself with Us //

So far we've discussed God's qualities that are entirely his own. They are not qualities that we possess. But there are attributes and character traits that God wants to share with us.

1. God's holiness. The word *holy* literally means "to cut" or "to separate." God is entirely unique or "set apart" from all of creation. He does everything right and good. He cannot lie, steal, cheat, or be unfaithful. He is morally pure and eternally righteous. He is the opposite of evil. It is impossible for God to sin.

We read of angelic beings who sing, "Holy, holy, holy is the LORD of Heaven's Armies!"[26] The triple emphasis on "holy" in this verse is a Hebrew literary technique. God is not just "holy,"

---

24 *Genesis 50:20, NASB.*

25 *Job 1:13; 2:6; see also 1 Corinthians 10:13.*

26 *Isaiah 6:3.*

or even "holy, holy," but he is "holy, holy, holy"—three times holy. The number three is a symbol of completion or perfection. So God's holiness is complete holiness, perfect holiness.

The holiness of God is the reason behind the cross of Jesus Christ. God cannot tolerate sin, because his nature is holy and just. Sin, therefore, demands punishment. But in his love, God sacrificed his own Son to pay for sin and thus provided a way for human beings to have a relationship with our holy God.

Because our God is holy, we are called to be holy also.[27] Holiness is a trait he wants to transfer to his children. Ultimately this is fulfilled through Christ's sacrifice and forgiveness, but practically it is exercised through our personal choice and obedience. Just as God justifies us (declares us righteous) in Christ, so also he sanctifies us (cleanses us) through his Spirit. This cleansing is often called "progressive sanctification," and even though it is the work of God in our lives, it is a process that believers participate in and "work out" as we follow Jesus.[28] A lifestyle of moral purity, ethical integrity, and sincere honesty demonstrates holiness in our lives.

2. God's love. One of the most famous verses in the New Testament is John 3:16, and it starts with the words "For God so loved . . . ." The word for "loved" in the original language is the Greek word *agape*. It is a stronger word than the common English use of *love*. We loosely say we love our dog, love chocolate, and love the beach, but *agape* is an unconditional commitment to an imperfect being. My feelings of love for my dog are conditional upon her not emitting atomic odors in my face, which she does quite often. But God loves you and does not stop (even when you emit atomic odors). *Agape* is the strongest possible type of love. Even though we disappoint God and naturally sin against him, he still loves us. He is committed to us. He is on our side.

In this sense, love is more like a verb than a noun. Love is active and by its very nature will be demonstrated to the one

27 *1 Peter 1:16.*

28 *Philippians 2:12-13, NIV.*

loved. Real love is filled with goodness and kindness and commit-ment. The extensive definition of love laid out in 1 Corinthians 13 is incredible: love is patient, kind, humble, joyful, truthful, endur-ing, persistent, faithful, hopeful, and full of belief, not to mention it doesn't keep score. That is certainly a bigger kind of love than most of us are used to receiving, let alone giving. But that is how God loves us. And it is how God wants us to love others. "Dear friends," John wrote, "since God loved us that much, we surely ought to love each other."[29]

Do you have a reputation for kindness? Are you known for your loyal love? How have you demonstrated your affection to your family lately? Maybe it's time to take your kids on that long-promised fishing trip. Maybe you should set aside work to give some focused attention to your spouse, not because it's your anniversary or Valentine's Day, but just because you love him or her. In loving others in small and large ways, we imitate our God, who is love.[30]

Everything Changes but God //

There are many more aspects to God. We haven't even finished exploring the tip of the iceberg of God's immensity. This survey should inspire us in our lifelong quest of painting the right pic-ture of God on our hearts. But there is one more attribute that I want to underscore before we conclude the chapter, and it affects every other attribute.

We live in a world of change. Mark Twain said, "The only person who likes change is a wet baby." But change is all around us. Some of us used to own these ancient artifacts called *vinyl albums.* These days albums are the stuff of DJs who spin records. We never wanted them to get scratched; now "scratching" is pretty much all they're used for. Two generations ago, most peo-ple didn't move more than fifty miles away from where they were born. A little more than a hundred years ago, people were put

29 *1 John 4:11.*
30 *1 John 4:8, 16.*

in prison if they couldn't pay their debts. The digital watch you wear on your wrist contains more computing power than existed in the whole world before 1961. In the 1950s, services provided by the U.S. government, such as the Post Office, seemed inefficient and laborious, but these days . . . Okay, that last one's a bad example.

In all of this change, however, God remains the same: "I am the LORD, and I do not change."[31]

This wonderful truth about God applies to every one of his other characteristics. He will always be present. He will never be without power. He will always be good. He will always love you in Christ. His majesty and glory will never cease. His grace and truth will always be available. He will never lose control. Everything changes . . . except God!

> ALL OF OUR ADMIRATION
> AND AFFECTION SHOULD BE
> CENTERED ON GOD,
> BECAUSE GOD IS THE ONLY ONE
> WORTHY OF ALL ADMIRATION
> AND AFFECTION. //

Worthy of Worship //

What is the picture of God now emerging from this survey of the Bible's teaching about God? We see that God is supreme and supremely sovereign. We see that he is all encompassing and all surpassing. We see that he is holy and just but also loving and merciful. We see that life and death and everything in between begins and ends with God.

Here is the most crucial point of application: If God is great and powerful, and if everything begins and ends with him, and if he desires a relationship with his creation, then what does this mean for our thoughts, words, and actions? In other

---

31 *Malachi 3:6.*

words, how does knowing all this and more about God affect our worship?

Everybody worships something. The worship switch is always set to On. Anything we derive pleasure from, anything we derive satisfaction from, anything we ascribe supreme worth to (be it family, friends, art, sex, music, sports, and so forth) can become the thing that we worship. But if by his very nature God is bigger and more powerful and more lasting than all of those things, then not only should our worship be tuned to him, but also our worship of him should be turned up to 11![32]

All of our admiration and affection should be centered on God, because God is the only one worthy of all admiration and affection. The Bible calls this combination of admiration and affection "glory," and God is frequently said to be doing things and saying things for the sake of his own glory. As one early Christian Q&A stated, the chief end of humanity is to glorify God and enjoy him forever.[33] Basically, the meaning of life is to wholeheartedly worship the giver and sustainer of life . . . and to enjoy doing so!

Our problems, no matter how big, are not bigger than God. No matter how long they last, they cannot outlast the eternal God. This is the God who makes uncensored grace so powerful, so freeing, so radical. Because he is truly holy, he has the power to truly forgive. Because he is truly powerful, he has the ability to change hearts. Because he is truly loving and truly sovereign, he has the power to draw us to himself and fulfill his vision for the redemption of the world. He isn't in heaven wringing his hands over the latest cultural shift. He's large and in charge. He has "royal power" and "rules all the nations."[34] Earth has its princes, but the universe has its God.

You might need a bigger wallet or purse—or heaven forbid, fellas, a bigger "man bag"—but do you need to change the picture of God that you carry?

---

32 *Apologies to Spinal Tap.*

33 *The Westminster Shorter Catechism, written in the 1640s.*

34 *Psalm 22:28.*

Discussion Questions

1. How do people formulate their perception of God or their personal beliefs?

2. How big is your God? How does this chapter increase your view of God?

3. How does the fact that God never changes affect you?

4. Read Philippians 4:13. How does knowing God's power and presence help you in your circumstances?

5. How can you practice the presence of God this week?

JESUS IS MORE THAN MY HOMEBOY//

CHAPTER .02

✳ ✳ ✳ Lately I feel like Jesus is everywhere and nowhere.

I see his image all over the place. He's on T-shirts, bobble-head dolls, and product packaging ranging from breath mints to jewelry. Just consider the magazine cover stories that always hit stores around Christmas and Easter. One journalist called this trend "Jesus Christ, Cover Star." One of the cover stories mentioned by that journalist was *U.S. News & World Report's* "In Search of the Real Jesus." (Apparently that reporter had lost him since writing a previous cover story titled "The Real Jesus."[1]) *Time* magazine called us to "Search for Jesus" and in a different year to "Search for Mary." *Newsweek* investigated "How Jesus Became Christ." And so on.

All the covers in the grocery store checkout line are like Jesus mug shots profiling the usual suspects, insisting we pick one out of the lineup. The challenge is that these writers paint very different pictures of Jesus. In one article he is a sage; in another, a philosopher or magician; in others, an idealistic Goody Two-shoes. Some see Jesus like an exalted John Lennon: he is a nice guy who would never hurt a fly, singing about peace in tinted circular glasses. Some have cast him in the role of celebrity kitsch, the groovy buddy adorning T-shirts that declare, "Jesus Is My Homeboy."

Shock rocker Marilyn Manson said, "Jesus was the first rock star. The cross is the biggest, greatest piece of merchandise in history, bigger than any concert T-shirt. And Jesus was the first dead rock star. Like Jim Morrison and Kurt Cobain and Jimi Hendrix, he became immortal by dying."[2]

---

1 Liz Cox Barrett, "Jesus Christ, Cover Star," Colombia Journalism Review, December 14, 2006, http://www.cjr.org/behind_the_news/jesus_christ_cover_star.php.

2 Marilyn Manson, "The Dead Rock Star," Rolling Stone, May 2003.

To some, Jesus is no more than a historical religious figure, much like Buddha or Moses or Muhammad. Others just wish he'd go away. Nirvana's Kurt Cobain claimed to have graffitied "God is gay!" and "Abort Christ" on cars and buildings.[3] And to many, "Jesus Christ" is just something you yell when you hit your thumb with a hammer.

Every show on the Discovery and History channels that deals with Jesus quotes lots of conflicting scholars and usually ends with more questions than answers, offering not-so-helpful statements like, "In the end, there are many faces of Jesus, but one thing is for certain: his followers will continue to see him differently as they follow him all over the world." And so not even television can make heads or tails of the most important figure in world history—which should not surprise us given that this is the same medium that brought us stellar programming like *Temptation Island* and *Jon & Kate Plus Seething Rage*.

Radical scholars get together and hash out which of Jesus' words they think we can trust. Emergent Christians write about how we need to reframe our vision of Jesus and his mission. Booksellers keep marketing the "new" and "controversial" thoughts on Jesus (most of which aren't new and in fact have already been discredited and discounted throughout church history).

Pollsters tell us that Jesus is doing pretty well among the public. His Q rating is off the charts. Apparently, 71 percent of Americans believe Jesus was the Son of God, while 70 percent believe he rose from the dead. Of course, the same 2008 Harris Poll that provided those results also shows that 44 percent of Americans believe in ghosts and 36 percent believe in UFOs.[4] So let's not revel in Jesus' superior market share just yet.

Clearly, when it comes to the subject of Jesus, there is a lot of discussion, a lot of fanfare, and a lot of confusion. Where can

---

3 Charles R. Cross, Heavier than Heaven: A Biography of Kurt Cobain (New York: Hyperion, 2002), 68.

4 Jennifer Harper, "Beliefs in God, UFOs Prevail," Washington Times, December 12, 2008, http://www.washington times.com/news/2008/dec/12/beliefs-in-god-ufos-prevail/.

we turn for some solidity when it comes to making sense of the Jesus Christ of the four Gospels?

The Creedal Christ //

The good news is that historic Christians were actually not all that confused about who Jesus claimed to be. The church fathers brought some clarity to the church's expression of faith in Jesus through the creeds. Creeds are a bit out of fashion these days. If you're like me, when you hear the word "creed," you first think of the Grammy Award–winning band with that name that peaked in the late 1990s. The band Creed is now famous for being one of the first results that pops up when you Google the phrase "worst band in the world." Creed is also a creepy old dude on the TV show *The Office*. Perhaps the word needs some modern rehab, and we can start by recalling its roots. Historically, a creed is a formal statement of belief.

One of the oldest creeds affirmed universally by Christians is the Nicene Creed. It says this about Jesus:

> We believe . . . in one Lord Jesus Christ, the only begotten Son of God, begotten of his Father before all works, God of God, Light of Light, very God of very God, begotten, not made, being of one substance with the Father; by whom all things were made; who for us and for our salvation came down from heaven, and was incarnate by the Holy Spirit of the virgin Mary, and was made man; and was crucified also for us under Pontius Pilate; he suffered and was buried; and on the third day he rose again according to the Scriptures, and ascended into heaven, and is seated at the right hand of the Father; and he shall come again, with glory, to judge both the living and the dead; whose kingdom shall have no end.

Because they believed the Gospels were historical documents reporting on a historical Jesus who said and did historical things, these early Christians believed some very *concrete* things about Jesus. Their beliefs were grounded in the Bible and history, so they were not blown about by the winds of sensationalist speculation. Their Jesus was no myth or icon built around hints and whispers, so their statements about him have a firmness that is of immense value to us today. Let's explore what historic Christianity affirms about Jesus.

What's in a Name? //

We are called Christians because we follow Jesus Christ. The name Jesus, which is actually a variation of Joshua, was a common name in the first century and meant "he will save." Jesus' last name, by the way, is not "Christ." (And his middle initial isn't H.) The word Christ is a Greek title that means "anointed one" and is the equivalent of the Hebrew title Messiah. Both Christ and Messiah were used to describe the one whom God would send to rescue Israel.

Names are very important in the Bible. Just ask Jacob, who wrestled with God and got named Israel, which means "struggles with God." Or Adam, whose name means (quite creatively) "man." Or Ponyboy, whose name means "my dad hated me." The very name of Jesus captures the longing of thousands of years for Israel's deliverance by the hand of God. The meaning of Jesus' name—"he will save"—encapsulates the promise God made in his covenant with his children. The Old Testament promised a hero who would come and rule the world through Israel. Listen to this prediction from Isaiah 9:6-7:

> *A child is born to us,*
> > *a son is given to us.*
> *The government will rest on his shoulders....*
> *His government and its peace*
> > *will never end.*
> *He will rule with fairness and justice from the throne of*
> > *his ancestor David*
> > > *for all eternity.*

JESUS TOOK THEM ON A TOUR OF
THE OLD TESTAMENT TO SHOW THAT
HIS LIFE, STYLE OF MINISTRY, CRUCIFIXION,
AND RESURRECTION WERE ALL
FORETOLD IN ITS PAGES. //

Israel fully expected a king to emerge from their country and rule. He would be the Messiah, the Christ, the anointed one. So when we say "Jesus Christ," we mean that the man Jesus was the anointed one of God, the Messiah. He is Jesus the Christ who was foretold in the Old Testament of the Bible.

Jesus' Life Was Foretold //

The Old Testament prophets, under the inspiration of God, foretold much that Jesus would go through when he came to earth. Seven hundred years before Jesus' birth, Micah prophesied that he would be born in Bethlehem. Isaiah prophesied that he would be born of a virgin. He also foretold that Jesus would not sin, would perform miracles, would be beaten and spat upon, and would be despised and rejected without defending himself.[5]

Likewise, David prophesied about Jesus. His Psalm 22 contains a prophecy that Jesus would be crucified and begins with a cry of the heart that Jesus quoted from the cross: "My God, my God why have you abandoned me?"[6] The psalm goes on to read:

> *My enemies surround me like a pack of dogs;*
> *an evil gang closes in on me.*
> *They have pierced my hands and feet.*
> *I can count all my bones.*
> *My enemies stare at me and gloat.*
> *They divide my garments among themselves*
> *and throw dice for my clothing.*[7]

---

5   Born in Bethlehem: Micah 5:2. Born of a virgin: Isaiah 7:14. Sinless: Isaiah 53:9. Miracles: Isaiah 35:5-6. Beaten
    and spat upon: Isaiah 50:6. Despised and rejected: Isaiah 53.

6   Psalm 22:1; see Mark 15:34.

7   Psalm 22:16-18.

The fascinating thing about this prophecy is that it was written hundreds of years before crucifixion was even invented. David also prophesied that Jesus would rise from the dead.[8]

There are many more prophecies in the Old Testament that were fulfilled by Christ.[9]

Jesus referred to these writings constantly as he began foretelling events of his life and death. To some guys walking on a road after his resurrection, he said, " 'When I was with you before, I told you that everything written about me in the law of Moses and the prophets and in the Psalms must be fulfilled.' Then he opened their minds to understand the Scriptures. And he said, 'Yes, it was written long ago that the Messiah would suffer and die and rise from the dead on the third day.' "[10] Jesus took them on a tour of the Old Testament to show that his life, style of ministry, crucifixion, and resurrection were all foretold in its pages.

People are still discovering Jesus in the Old Testament today. When I first met Andrew, he explained that he was a committed Jew, but he had been reading his Bible and had some questions. He opened his Tanakh (the Jewish Old Testament), turned to Isaiah 53, and read this passage aloud to me:

> He was pierced for our rebellion,
>> crushed for our sins.
> He was beaten so we could be whole.
>> He was whipped so we could be healed.[11]

Andrew looked up at me with absolute sincerity and asked, "Who could this be about, if it isn't about Jesus?"

I smiled and said, "That's my question exactly."

He then turned to some other passages that seemed to point to Jesus.

---

8 Psalm 16:10.

9 An entire catalog of these fulfilled predictions can be found in Herbert Lockyer, All the Messianic Prophecies of the Bible (Grand Rapids, MI: Zondervan, 1988).

10 Luke 24:44-46.

11 Isaiah 53:5.

Andrew was a guy who was literally reading his way to faith in the Old Testament prophecies concerning Jesus. He wasn't searching for Jesus initially, but he discovered him there and learned that Jesus was searching for *him*. He continued to study, and later he and all his immediate family placed their faith and trust in Jesus.

Jesus Is God //

Famous fashion designer Gianni Versace once said, "I believe in God, but I'm not the kind of religious person who goes to church, who believes in the fairy tale of Jesus born in the stable with the donkey. . . . I'm not stupid. I can't believe that God, with all the power that he has, had to have himself born in a stable. It wouldn't have been comfortable."[12] This from a guy who lived so luxuriously that even Madonna said she was embarrassed by how much money he spent. But what Versace found irrational and inconceivable was the redeeming "discomfort" that we call the Incarnation.

The story of the Bible is about God's faithfulness in relationship to his creation, and the New Testament story is one of God going to an extreme to maintain this relationship. He came to earth in the person of Jesus Christ, even though it was not comfortable. This is the great "emptying" of self that Paul wrote about:

> *Though he was God,*
> *he did not think of equality with God*
> *as something to cling to.*
> *Instead, he gave up his divine privileges;*
> *he took the humble position of a slave*
> *and was born as a human being.*
> *When he appeared in human form,*
> *he humbled himself in obedience to God*
> *and died a criminal's death on a cross.*[13]

---

12 *Quoted in Andre Lee, "The Emperor of Dreams," New Yorker, July 28, 1997.*

13 *Philippians 2:6-8.*

The language here, and the knowledge that inspires it, goes beyond a good man embracing peace and martyrdom. It is about the God of the universe willingly relinquishing his right to comfort and power.

The Bible teaches that Jesus is co-equal with the Father and the Holy Spirit. This is known as the deity of Christ. Jesus, in essence, said that to know me is to know God, to see me is to see God, to believe in me is to believe in God, to receive me is to receive God, to hate me is to hate God, and to honor me is to honor God.[14]

The Jewish leaders plotted to kill Jesus because he was "making himself equal with God." Later, as Jesus was teaching, the people began to pick up rocks with which to stone him. The God-man refused to back down, saying, "At my Father's direction I have done many good works. For which one are you going to stone me?" They replied, "We're stoning you not for any good work, but for blasphemy! You, a mere man, claim to be God."[15]

JESUS CLAIMED TO BE GOD,
AND THIS CLAIM RESULTED
IN EXTREME POLARIZATION AMONG
HIS AUDIENCE—SOMETHING JUST
BEING "NICE" RARELY DOES. //

There was no confusion in the minds of Jesus' hearers over what he was claiming. If there had been, Jesus certainly had the opportunity to clear it up. But he didn't, because despite his rejection of their violence, he knew he was guilty of their allegation. But he wasn't guilty of their charge of blasphemy, because it's not blasphemy for God himself to claim to be God. As a good religious Jew, Jesus knew that any mortal man claiming to be equal with God would be committing blasphemy—indeed

14 Know: John 8:19; 14:7. See: John 12:45; 14:9. Believe: John 12:44; 14:1. Receive: Mark 9:37. Hate: John 15:23.
    Honor: John 5:23.
15 John 5:18; 10:32-33.

a capital offense. He knew the implications of his own implicit and explicit claims to deity. This would be a ridiculous assertion for just anyone to make. If you had a teacher who claimed to be the Almighty, you would check him or her into a mental health clinic as soon as possible. No matter how well you liked this person, or how moral this person's teachings were, you would still think that he or she was a few fries short of a Happy Meal!

Even most atheists wouldn't say that Jesus was insane, and hardly anyone would say he was a liar. Jesus claimed to be God, and this claim resulted in extreme polarization among his audience—something just being "nice" rarely does. Those around Jesus reacted with shock, scandalized by his audacity . . . or they followed him in reckless faith.

Paul brought clarity to the Christian perspective in the first chapter of Colossians:

> *Christ is the visible image of the invisible God.*
> *He existed before anything was created and*
>   *is supreme over all creation,*
> *for through him God created everything*
>   *in the heavenly realms and on earth.*
> *He made the things we can see*
>   *and the things we can't see—*
> *such as thrones, kingdoms, rulers, and authorities in the*
> *unseen world.*
>   *Everything was created through him and for him.*
> *He existed before anything else,*
>   *and he holds all creation together.*
> *Christ is also the head of the church,*
>   *which is his body.*
> *He is the beginning,*
>   *supreme over all who rise from the dead.*
>   *So he is first in everything.*
> *For God in all his fullness*
>   *was pleased to live in Christ,*

> *and through him God reconciled*
> *everything to himself.*
> *He made peace with everything in heaven and on earth*
> *by means of Christ's blood on the cross.*[16]

The claim that Jesus is God in the flesh is one of the clearest distinguishing points between Christianity and other religions. Most religions acknowledge that Jesus was a good teacher, but only Christianity bows to him as Lord of lords and King of kings. Judaism, Islam, Mormonism, and other religions teach that Jesus had good qualities, some even acknowledging that he was a prophet, and a few that he was in some sense a divine personality. But none of these religions believe that Jesus is fully and eternally God, existing equally with the Father and the Spirit. The teaching of the deity of Christ is unique to Christianity and foundational to the Christian faith.

Jesus Became a Guy //

Deity became dude. Jesus, who existed as God in eternity past, left his exalted place and stepped into this world in a human body for a brief lifetime of thirty-something years. He then returned to the heavenly realm in his glorified human body. In foregoing the full array of his deity, Jesus set aside some of his attributes (such as omnipresence) so that he could become fully human. Living on earth as both fully God and fully human, he paid the penalty for our sins.

The act of God becoming man is known as the Incarnation. God *incarnate* means God "in the flesh." The Christmas story kicks off the Incarnation with Jesus' miraculous conception and birth.

According to the Gospel of Luke, the angel Gabriel was sent by God to the town of Nazareth, where he announced to a young woman named Mary that she would give birth to a Son, and that she was to name him Jesus, and that his kingdom wouldn't end. It wasn't exactly news you could put on a Hallmark card.

---

16 *Colossians 1:15-20.*

DEITY BECAME DUDE. JESUS, WHO EXISTED AS GOD IN ETERNITY PAST, LEFT HIS EXALTED PLACE AND STEPPED INTO THIS WORLD IN A HUMAN BODY FOR A BRIEF LIFETIME OF THIRTY-SOMETHING YEARS.

Mary, as you can imagine, was not initially excited. She had more basic things in mind. "But how can this happen?" she asked. "I am a virgin."[17]

The angel explained, "The Holy Spirit will come upon you, and the power of the Most High will overshadow you. So the baby to be born will be holy, and he will be called the Son of God."[18]

Jesus was born of a virgin. This is an important Christian belief because it positions us from the outset to correctly answer the question of who Jesus is. Was he without sin? Was he uniquely the Son of God? These questions point back to the virgin birth.

Larry King was once asked who he would like to interview if he could sit down with anyone who had ever lived. He replied, "Jesus." What would King ask him? "Are you indeed virgin born?"[19] He knew that the answer to that one question would answer all the others, and this is why historic Christianity has held firmly to a belief in this teaching.

Jesus grew up in Nazareth obeying his earthly parents and learning a trade as a carpenter. When he became a man of thirty, he began his ministry as an itinerant preacher and rabbi. He selected a group of twelve disciples out of the crowds who followed him, and he invested in them as their teacher and friend. For three years he taught and healed as they roamed the towns and countryside of Palestine, also solving mysteries and getting into kung fu fights. (Okay, I made that last part up. But wouldn't it be awesome if it were true?)

Jesus Never Sinned //

One important reason for the virgin birth is that it affirms that Jesus was conceived by the Holy Spirit and did not inherit the original sin of Adam. Jesus lived in this fallen, sinful world and yet he did not sin. Peter, one of Jesus' closest friends, claimed, "He never sinned, nor ever deceived anyone." John said, "Jesus

---

17 *Luke 1:34.*

18 *Luke 1:35.*

19 *As quoted in Ravi Zacharias,* Jesus among Other Gods *(Nashville: Thomas Nelson, 2002), 38.*

came to take away our sins, and there is no sin in him." Paul also said that Jesus "never sinned."[20]

As a man, Jesus experienced the reality of life. He saw poverty and sickness. He felt joy and sorrow. He danced and sang and itched and got hungry. His experience in this world was deeply authentic. From the scrapes and bruises of childhood play to blisters in the woodworking shop to the angst of puberty to every temptation and into the pain of death, he never crossed over the line into dishonesty or immorality or rebellion. He was confronted with every opportunity to choose wrong over right, but in the power and purity of his unique character, he always chose the right thing to do.

Thanks to Jesus, we never need to view God as a deity who lives in some faraway corner of the cosmos, clueless about what we're going through. Jesus understands perfectly because he has been there.

You may wonder, "How can Jesus understand if he never gave in to temptation?"

Temptation exists in the tension of desiring to do something sinful, not in actually doing it. Once we give in to temptation, we often aren't tempted again in that way for a period of time, maybe minutes or maybe days or months. Jesus, by contrast, lived in that tension of temptation continually but never caved. He understands temptation at a level none of the rest of us can. The author of Hebrews said:

Since we have a great High Priest who has entered heaven, Jesus the Son of God, let us hold firmly to what we believe. This High Priest of ours understands our weaknesses, for he faced all of the same testings we do, yet he did not sin. So let us come boldly to the throne of our gracious God. There we will receive his mercy, and we will find grace to help us when we need it most.[21]

---

20 *1 Peter 2:22; 1 John 3:5; 2 Corinthians 5:21.*

21 *Hebrews 4:14-16.*

When you struggle with your own human weaknesses, know that God understands. You can boldly go to him because Jesus knows what it is like to be human. He faced the difficult challenges that you do, wants to help you make the right choices, and wants to forgive you when you make the wrong choices.

Jesus' Miracles Rocked //

During his ministry, Jesus continually performed miracles that defied the laws of nature. These were not some podunk illusionist's lame sleight of hand. Jesus' works were total showstoppers, incredible acts of God. They attracted the crowds and confounded the critics. These astounding miracles forced people to recognize that Jesus was not an ordinary teacher. Only the promised Messiah from God could have power over creation like this.

The Gospels record thirty-four of Jesus' miracles. There are also fifteen texts (excluding parallels) that describe Jesus' miracle working in summary fashion.[22] And then we have miracles of which Jesus was the object: his birth, baptism, transfiguration, resurrection, and ascension. The Gospel of John ends with these words: "Jesus also did many other things. If they were all written down, I suppose the whole world could not contain the books that would be written."[23] His miracles shook people up and gave them pause to consider Jesus' claims.

In his book *Miracles*, C. S. Lewis explores these amazing feats. Lewis, a scholar in medieval and classic literature and an expert in ancient myths, was surprised that Christ's miraculous stories do not contain the usual elements of other mythical literature. There is no trickery in Jesus' miracles, none of the cosmological "messing around" typical among the precocious gods of myth and legends. The Gospels don't mention boats becoming goddesses or men being turned into bears. The miracles in

---

22 *Robert H. Stein,* Jesus the Messiah: A Survey of the Life of Christ *(Downers Grove, IL: InterVarsity Press,*
     1996), 143.
23 *John 21:25.*

the Gospels create their own category, and Lewis organized them into two subcategories—the Old Creation and the New Creation.

In miracles of the Old Creation, Jesus operated within natural laws but skipped some of the natural processes. Every farmer knows that if you plant wheat it will grow and you will have a harvest. There is basic reproduction. When Jesus fed the five thousand, he skipped the natural processes of reproduction. When Jesus multiplied the fish, he did something that God does in the oceans every day, but he did it quickly and uniquely. When Jesus calmed the storm on the sea, he did what God has done for years. All storms that are not currently raging have been stilled by God, but in this case it happened immediately and instantly. Lewis writes, "If God creates a miraculous [embryo] in the body of a virgin, it does not proceed to break any laws. The laws at once take it over. Nature is ready. Pregnancy follows, according to all the normal laws, and nine months later a child is born."[24]

There are also miracles of the New Creation. By this Lewis means miracles that are a foretaste of the nature that lies in the future. For example, Jesus walked on water. Water was not made for humans to walk on. Another example is when Jesus raised his friend Lazarus from the dead. People who have been dead for days do not come back to life (despite the awesomeness of zombie movies).[25]

By performing miracles of Old Creation and New Creation, Jesus displayed his authority over *all* creation and also testified to himself as the bridge between the fallenness of the old and the redemption of the new. The miracles, then, were not merely displays of power and authority, although they certainly were those things, and incredibly so. They were living pictures of the transformation and salvation that only Jesus could bring.

And this is a salvation that Jesus *still* brings, as he continues performing miracles in people's lives today.

---

24 C. S. Lewis, Miracles *(New York: HarperCollins, 2001), 59–60.*

25 *Matthew 14:22-36; John 11:38-44.*

SIMPLY PUT, HE DIED
ON THE'CROSS TO SAVE US.
THE LOVE OF GOD IS SUPREMELY
EXPRESSED IN THIS
ONE ACT OF HISTORY. //

Jesus: On a Mission from God //

The Blues Brothers weren't the only ones on a mission from God. The motto and mission of Christ is found in Luke 19:10: "The Son of Man came to seek and save those who are lost." Jesus was born into this world and clothed with human flesh to live and model life for us, but also to die on a cross and be the perfect, sinless sacrifice for humanity. He came, not for those who have it all together, but for the messed-up and the down-and-out and the vast array of earth's losers. He did not come to enhance human success but to reverse humanity's epic failure.

Simply put, he died on the cross to save us.

The love of God is supremely expressed in this one act of history. As Paul said, "God showed his great love for us by sending Christ to die for us while we were still sinners."[26]

Without Jesus there would be no salvation. God the Father sent God the Son to die in your place on a lonely cross. The events of his death are covered thoroughly in each of the four Gospels. The Gospels, indeed, devote nearly one third of their material to the last week of Jesus' life. Why? Because that's how important Jesus' death is.

Through a Thursday night and Friday morning, Jesus endured three Jewish trials or hearings and three Roman trials. After a total of six trials in the short span of eighteen hours, Jesus was sentenced to be crucified.

There were all kinds of breaches of justice in Jesus' trials. Mark Moore lists eleven of these infractions:

---

26 *Romans 5:8.*

1. He was arrested through a bribe (i.e., blood money).
2. He was arrested without a clear charge.
3. Trials could not be held at night or on feast days.
4. They used physical force to try to intimidate Jesus during the trial.
5. False witnesses offered conflicting testimony against him.
6. Witnesses were not supposed to testify in the presence of each other.
7. Jesus was asked to incriminate himself, which he really didn't do!
8. Jesus was not given the opportunity to cross-examine the witnesses.
9. The high priest never asked for a vote from the Sanhedrin, which should have started with the youngest and gone to the oldest.
10. He was charged with blasphemy and temple violation at his Jewish trial, but the charges were changed at his civil trial to claiming to be king, causing disturbances, and refusing to pay taxes.
11. He was convicted and executed the same day as his trial.[27]

Those are the ingredients for a serious mistrial and corruption of justice. Somebody get Johnny Cochran! (Yes, Johnny Cochran is dead, but we all know that's no speed bump for Jesus.)

Jesus never objected, though. He willingly submitted to it all. After his sham conviction, Jesus was executed between two thieves. They were thrown together in some of the most grueling circumstances invented by human beings. They endured torture side by side. They were crucified at a place called Golgotha, or in Latin, *Calvary*. Both words mean "the place of the skull." We don't know why the place was named that. The Jews would not have

---

27 *Mark Moore*, The Chronological Life of Christ, vol. 2, From Galilee to Glory *(Joplin, MO: College Press, 1997), 267–8.*

allowed skulls to collect outside their city. Perhaps the formation of the hill looked like a skull. Or perhaps it was just known as a place where people died.

Jesus was crucified at about nine in the morning, and he remained on the cross until three in the afternoon. From noon till three, there was darkness over all the land. The Gospels document Jesus speaking seven times during those six terrible hours. The first thing he said was "Father, forgive them, for they don't know what they are doing."[28] This means Jesus' first words from the cross were not about the excruciating pain or looming death. They were about you and me.

You've probably figured this out already, but crucifixion is a gruesome way to die. Our modern equivalents in the world of capital punishment—the gas chamber and the electric chair—are tame compared to the cross.

For one thing, lethal injection and the electric chair are used to hasten death. But crucifixion was like self-maintained torture. The pain was excruciating, yes. It was bloody and gruesome and grotesque. But the design of crucifixion was such that the condemned typically suffocated. Dr. William Edwards writes:

> Adequate exhalation required lifting the body by pushing up on the feet and by flexing the elbows. . . . However, this maneuver would place the entire weight of the body on the tarsals [a part of the foot] and would produce searing pain. . . . Muscle cramps and paresthesias [tingling numbness] of the outstretched and uplifted arms would add to the discomfort. As a result, each respiratory effort would become agonizing and tiring and lead eventually to asphyxia.[29]

So crucifixion prolonged death, adding time and an exponentially increasing amount of pain.

---

28 *Mark 15:25, 33; Luke 23:34.*

29 *William Edwards et al., "On the Physical Death of Jesus Christ,"* Journal of the American Medical Association *255, no. 11 (1986): 1461.*

And on top of the agony, the ancient act of crucifixion added the shame of public display. Modern executions are private, conducted in secluded prison rooms in the presence of a limited number of select witnesses. Crucifixion was public, the condemned exposed to the prying eyes, the jeering mouths, and even the abusive hands of onlookers.

The act of crucifixion was so gruesome, in fact, that the Gospel writers gave no detail of the process other than the one word itself: "crucified." All they needed was that one word—in that era it painted the picture of horror. As Martin Hengel reminds us, the word itself was considered vulgar, not to be uttered in polite company.[30] Jesus suffered so intensely, and his followers sympathized so deeply, that they could not bring themselves to mention it in any words but the briefest.

R. C. Sproul noted how strange it is that we glorify the cross. We wear it on jewelry and place it on walls in our churches. This symbol of legalized torture became the primary symbol of the Christian faith. Sproul writes, "I wonder if the Romans had chosen to hang, or to behead, or to mutilate, or to shoot, would we sing of the precious old rope? Would we talk of the sweet machete, or the blessed .357 Magnum? Think about the moving factor of Christ's love. Christ's love changes everything it touches, even a tool to execute someone."

His love transformed those crossbeams into the very place where God's justice and forgiveness collided. John wrote, "We know what real love is because Jesus gave up his life for us."[31]

After this act of outrageous love Jesus was placed in a tomb, but early on Sunday he rose again!

You Can't Keep a God-Man Down //
Millions of skeptics have struggled with the empty tomb. In the spring of 2007, buzz abounded in the media about a

30 *Martin Hengel,* Crucifixion in the Ancient World and the Folly of the Message of the Cross *(Minneapolis: Fortress, 1977),* 9–10.

31 1 John 3:16.

JESUS POURED HIS
LOVE OUT FOR THE CRACK
ADDICTS, THE STRIPPERS,
THE BOOKIES, AND THE
PETTY THIEVES OF HIS DAY.

documentary called *The Lost Tomb of Jesus* that aired on the Discovery Channel. The documentary's subjects claimed they had found a tomb that might have belonged to Jesus. Yet the information in the broadcast came from relics removed back in 1980 from a construction site in Jerusalem. Workers at that time discovered an ancient burial place and removed ten ossuaries, or bone boxes.

The show droned on for a couple hours, looking at these bone boxes and their indistinct inscriptions. Was Jesus' resurrection a hoax? Had the workers found the tomb of Jesus? In short, no.

The frustrating thing about *The Lost Tomb of Jesus* is that virtually every distinguished archaeologist who examined it rejected the documentary makers' claims. Experts like Amos Kloner, the guy who supervised the original discovery in 1980 as an archeologist over the Jerusalem District, are a part of the skepticism. Kloner says, "It makes a great story for a TV film, but it's impossible. It's nonsense."[32]

Joe Zias, the curator at Jerusalem's Rockefeller Museum for twenty-five years and the guy who personally numbered the bone boxes, said of *The Lost Tomb of Jesus's* director, "He's pimping off the Bible. . . . Projects like these make a mockery of the archeological profession."[33]

For thousands of years, people have tried to get their mind around the empty tomb in Jerusalem. Peter struggled with it when he first came to the tomb, and Thomas had his doubts, but later Jesus appeared to comfort them.

There were eyewitnesses to Jesus' resurrection, people who recorded the event for posterity, and their testimony has been preserved to this day in our Bible. Beyond that, millions of people every year all over the world experience inner spiritual transformation when they begin to trust and follow the risen Christ. And this phenomenon continues to baffle the

---

32 Quoted in Brent Bozell, "What Bones of Jesus?" Townhall.com, February 28, 2007, http://townhall.com/ columnists/BrentBozell/2007/02/28/what_bones_of_jesus.

33 Ibid.

skeptics who think this whole deal should have died out a long time ago.

We're on a Mission from God //

After Jesus' resurrection, he spent parts of a forty-day period with his followers and appeared in Jerusalem and the surrounding area to women and to the two guys on the road to Emmaus. He also appeared to his disciples several times, to five hundred followers at one time, and to James.[34]

He appeared again to his disciples in Jerusalem and told them that they were to be his witnesses. Then he ascended. "As they strained to see him rising into heaven, two white-robed men suddenly stood among them. 'Men of Galilee,' they said, 'why are you standing here staring into heaven? Jesus has been taken from you into heaven, but someday he will return from heaven in the same way you saw him go!' "[35]

The disciples were standing there in awe as Jesus had vanished into heaven. With their mouths open and their eyes looking skyward, the angel said to them, "What are you standing around for?" The implication for us, as I read the text, is that it's time to get busy. Jesus will return, but for now we'd better get on with being his witnesses.

Consequently, we are all called to reach out to others and share our faith in Jesus. We are commanded to care for people and meet their needs. There were times when Jesus was sad and times when he was angry, but most of the time he saw the hurt and the pain that he alone could heal, and his heart welled up with compassion and love. In fact, the number-one emotional response of Jesus mentioned in the Gospels is compassion.[36] He wept at the death of his friend Lazarus.[37] Even though he was moments away from restoring life to his friend, Jesus still

---

34 *Acts 1:3; Matthew 28:1-10; Luke 24:13-35; John 20:19-24, 21:1-23; 1 Corinthians 15:6-7.*

35 *Acts 1:10-11.*

36 B. B. Warfield, The Person and Work of Christ, *ed. by Samuel G. Craig (Philadelphia: Presbyterian & Reformed Publishing, 1950), 96.*

37 *John 11:35.*

allowed the feelings of grief to overwhelm his soul and he stood with the family and wept.

Jesus made friends with those who were rejected by the crowds—the marginalized and the downtrodden, the poor and the diseased. The so-called sinners and tax collectors, even the prostitutes, found a friend in Jesus. The people on the edges of life, those of us who are messy, the ones the church has the hardest time reaching and keeping—those are the very people Jesus gravitated to. Despite and against the criticism of the religious leaders, Jesus allowed his compassion for people to lead him into relationships of help and healing. And so Jesus poured his love out for the crack addicts, the strippers, the bookies, and the petty thieves of his day.

This is astounding when we consider that Jesus was sinless but constantly surrounded by sin and sinful people. Sin violently opposed his very character. Everywhere he turned, he saw the effects of injustice and hate. It would have been easy for Jesus to haul off and blast people for their mistakes. He had more right than anyone to take a political and moral stand, to picket on the street, to organize protests, and to publicly attack individuals. Rather than being filled with disdain, however, he was filled with love.

If Jesus was the most spiritually mature person to ever live, then he stands as *the* model for what a spiritual life looks like. He remained approachable to outsiders and the hurting. His life reveals to me that the more spiritually mature I am, the more approachable I will be to people who feel far from God. As my spiritual maturity increases, my approachability should increase.[38]

IF JESUS WAS THE MOST SPIRITUALLY MATURE PERSON TO EVER LIVE, THEN HE STANDS AS *THE* MODEL FOR WHAT A SPIRITUAL LIFE LOOKS LIKE. //

38 *Thanks to John Ortberg for this insight.*

It is a sad indictment that many outside the faith don't feel as if they can approach Christians. In Jesus' day, some of the least approachable people were the religious leaders. They reeked of self-righteousness and judgment. Yet Jesus' life should give us pause. Let's ask ourselves the following questions:

- Am I truly approachable to all kinds of people?
- Am I open to relationships with all kinds of people?
- Do I have the compassion of Jesus for those who are hurting or disillusioned?
- Am I compelled by compassion?
- Is my compassion evident to others?

Let's not forget, though, that discipleship is not just a personal endeavor. It is designed to be lived out in community. When Jesus gave us the Great Commission, he wasn't strictly speaking to individual followers but to the church. As the body of Christ, we are to be about God's business. So these questions and the implications of the answers must apply to our churches as well. Who and what do our churches exist for? Are they known as safe places for the broken and the confused? Are they places where it's okay to not be okay? Are they places of hope and joy? As we maintain conviction of sin, are we teaching the good news, or are we teaching a spirit of condemnation under the law?

In short, how like Jesus is our discipleship and our community of disciples? If Jesus showed up, would he recognize what was going on as something he began?

These questions, and others like them, are ones that lately I've been asking more and more. The church I serve is far from perfect, and we have plenty of room to improve in this area. I pray that as we reflect on these questions we'll move toward being more a part of the solution as we share God's uncensored grace and truth in an uncompromising way. If we do this, we'll create cultures of belonging where people can experience the life-changing message of Jesus. We'll continue to be his witnesses.

Discussion Questions

1. *How was Jesus portrayed in your home growing up?*

2. *What do these verses teach about Jesus?*
   - *Romans 1:2-5*
   - *Colossians 2:9*

3. *Jesus wept, laughed, and got angry. How is the biblical description of Jesus different from the one portrayed by pop culture?*

4. *Read Hebrews 4:15. How does the fact that Jesus understands real human life affect your relationship with him? How does it make you feel?*

5. *Read Romans 8:29. How is God transforming you to be like Jesus?*

(HOLY)
GHOST
STORY//

✳ ✳ ✳ When I was a kid, I would hear people talking about "the Holy Ghost." That always confused me. The only ghosts I knew about were in movies like *Ghostbusters* or cartoons like *Casper the Friendly Ghost*. I watched ghosts chasing Scooby-Doo and Shaggy, so I guessed the Holy Ghost was a spook who chased church people around.

Later, as a new Christ follower, I learned that the term Holy Ghost was from an older translation of the Bible and that Holy Spirit was another way of describing him. But that didn't make the idea any less spooky. The terminology and the concept of the Holy Spirit, like those in the subject of the spiritual gifts, remained strange and unfamiliar to me. But as I grew in my faith, I learned that the Spirit of God is not like some Ghost of Christmas Past but rather is the Helper who lives within me.

There is lots of confusion about the Holy Spirit today, not least because he has become a caricature or is thought of as some kind of ethereal force or power. The Holy Spirit has become a concept, rather than a person, and is used in all sorts of spiritual descriptions, even vague ones. In a letter to the editor of *Rolling Stone*, for instance, A. J. Arendt wrote, "I am now convinced that Bono [of U2] is God and the Edge is the Holy Spirit." No doubt Arendt is acknowledging the spiritual substance of U2's music, but he's also irreverently co-opting sacred names for the purpose of tribute. Most are confused enough about the Holy Spirit without picturing the Edge playing guitar when they think of him. Many even in the church tend to treat the Holy Spirit like some impersonal, mystical "thing" used by God, like the force from *Star Wars* or something. But the real Holy Spirit is not so flexible of an identity.

THE HOLY SPIRIT IS HERE TO
COME ALONGSIDE YOU, TO GUIDE YOU,
OPEN YOUR UNDERSTANDING TO TRUTH,
REPAIR YOUR HEART, FILL YOU WITH VIRTUE,
AND EMPOWER YOU FOR EFFECTIVE
INFLUENCE IN THE LIVES OF OTHERS. //

The framers of the Nicene Creed recognized the Spirit's distinctive personhood and personality when they wrote, "We believe in the Holy Spirit, the Lord, the giver of Life, who proceeds from the Father and the Son. With the Father and the Son he is worshipped and glorified. He has spoken through the Prophets." These ancient Christians could see from the testimony of Scripture that the correct question isn't really "*What* is the Holy Spirit?" but rather "*Who* is the Holy Spirit?"

Just before Jesus went to the cross and then to heaven, he promised his followers that the Father would send someone else to help them. This someone else is the Holy Spirit. Jesus said, "The Helper, the Holy Spirit, whom the Father will send in My name, He will teach you all things, and bring to your remembrance all things that I said to you."[1]

The basic idea behind the Greek term for "Helper" is "one who is called alongside." The Holy Spirit is here to come alongside you, to guide you, open your understanding to truth, repair your heart, fill you with virtue, and empower you for effective influence in the lives of others. His ultimate aim is to point you to Jesus. The Holy Spirit is your number-one Helper, your Counselor, your Comforter, your Encourager.

No Expiration Dates //
The Old Testament is full of references to the Spirit of God. In those days, the Holy Spirit did not take up residency in a follower of God. When God wanted to work through an individual, the Holy Spirit would "come upon" that person, an event that is

---

1   *John 14:26,* NKJV.

sometimes referred to as "being filled with the Spirit."

The Spirit of God would so overwhelm a follower with power and presence that extraordinary feats of service would result. Joseph is a good example. Because Joseph could interpret dreams, he was recognized by the Pharaoh as one who had the Spirit of God in him. Joseph basically became the vice president of Egypt because of the Holy Spirit's provision and guidance. Similarly, prophets such as Isaiah and Ezekiel gave their prophecies when the Holy Spirit came upon them. In doing so, God revealed truth directly to his people without the use of the Scriptures.[2]

King David was well aware of the Holy Spirit's power in his rise to the throne of Israel. The Spirit of God had helped him as a warrior to conquer the nations and as a songwriter to pen psalms of worship. When he sinned against God, David thought God would remove his Spirit from him, as he had done with David's predecessor, Saul. So David pleaded with God as he prayed for forgiveness in Psalm 51:10-11:

> *Create in me a clean heart, O God.*
> *Renew a loyal spirit within me.*
> *Do not banish me from your presence,*
> *and don't take your Holy Spirit from me.*

This marks a crucial difference in the workings of the Spirit today compared to the Old Testament spiritual economy. Today the Spirit of God indwells every believer at the time of salvation. We never have to pray the prayer David prayed. We have the comfort and assurance that the Holy Spirit is always within us. This is God's promise fulfilled in the new covenant of Christ.

While we may grieve the Spirit or diminish our own assurance through doubt and sin, the Spirit's continual operation preserves the seed of salvation in us. Paul described the Spirit's

2   *See Genesis 37-50.*

irrevocable presence this way: "The Spirit is God's guarantee that he will give us the inheritance he promised and that he has purchased us to be his own people. He did this so we would praise and glorify him."[3]

The Holy Spirit is God's guarantee of his own promise of his Spirit. And all God's promises are true and good. There are no expiration dates!

Jesus went so far as to say that it was good that he ascend back to heaven so that we could have the Spirit. "It is best for you that I go away," he said to his disciples, "because if I don't, the Advocate won't come. If I do go away, then I will send him to you."[4]

And Jesus kept his promise. A few days later, after Jesus had ascended into heaven, the followers of Christ were huddled together, waiting and praying in Jerusalem. The remarkable account of what happened as Jesus kept his promise about sending the Holy Spirit is found in Acts 2:1-4:

> On the day of Pentecost all the believers were meeting together in one place. Suddenly, there was a sound from heaven like the roaring of a mighty windstorm, and it filled the house where they were sitting. Then, what looked like flames or tongues of fire appeared and settled on each of them. And everyone present was filled with the Holy Spirit and began speaking in other languages, as the Holy Spirit gave them this ability.

Have you ever experienced a tornado or gusts of wind that shook your house? On that day at the beginning of the church, out of heaven came a loud rushing wind that filled the place where Jesus' friends were staying. Then above them something like a flame appeared and began to spread onto each of them. As in the Old Testament, the Spirit of God came upon God's followers and evidenced his presence with something remarkable. This time it

---

3 *Ephesians 1:14.*

4 *John 16:7.*

was the ability to speak in a foreign language and be understood by the visitors in Jerusalem from foreign countries.

Remember, it was the Day of Pentecost, and Jews from around the known world had gathered in Jerusalem. It was a strategic moment to spread the good news of the risen Christ. The disciples would not have been able to pull this off in their own human abilities. There were no postcards to send out, no MySpace bulletins, no viral videos to e-mail. They could not communicate to so many foreigners, let alone gather the crowd in the first place, but with the help of the Holy Spirit, they had power and opportunity like never before.

In the same way, God's Spirit can empower you to accomplish God's task.

Now let's look at some key traits of the Holy Spirit.

The Divine Spirit //

As we have already said, historic Christianity teaches that the Spirit is co-equal with the Father and the Son. The Spirit of God was present at the formation of time and space. He existed before the world was created. He has all the same characteristics that the Father and the Son do. He is all powerful and ever present. He has all knowledge and wisdom. He is kind and loving. He is equal in every way to the Father and the Son even though he has a different ministry role.

The Son of God, not the Spirit of God, died on the cross. The Son is the head of the church, and the Spirit distributes spiritual gifts within the church. Each person within the Trinity is equal, but they function differently. There is one God but there are three Persons.

THE HOLY SPIRIT IS YOUR
NUMBER-ONE HELPER,
YOUR COUNSELOR,
YOUR COMFORTER,
YOUR ENCOURAGER. //

The Delivery Room //

When Jesus was asked about the process of salvation, he said, "I tell you the truth, unless you are born again, you cannot see the Kingdom of God."[5]

The man to whom Jesus was talking, Nicodemus, did not understand what Jesus was saying. He questioned him further, thinking that the idea of two births was ridiculous.

Jesus explained, "I assure you, no one can enter the Kingdom of God without being born of water and the Spirit. Humans can reproduce only human life, but the Holy Spirit gives birth to spiritual life."[6]

It fascinates me that Jesus used the metaphor of birth to represent spiritual transformation. The physical birth of a child is an amazing miracle. Just before our son Ethan was born, our doctor looked at me and asked if I'd like to deliver the baby. I said what any God-fearing person would say: "No!" I was thinking, *You take care of your business and I'll take care of mine. I'll pray for you!*

Then I looked over at my wife, and I could tell by her eyes that she wanted me to do this. So I suited up and put the gloves on, and when the moment came, I got to be the first person to touch our son and hold him up. It was the most amazing experience. I was overcome with joy. I stood in awe at all the complexities and details and millions of synchronized mini-miracles involved in God's creating a life!

But as amazing and beautiful as natural birth is, spiritual birth is even more so. Natural birth thrusts an infant into a world of colors, smells, shapes, and temperature adjustments. New birth also opens up a whole new world, the world of the spirit. Natural birth is the beginning of years of growth and maturity. Spiritual birth is the beginning of freedom to *real* life, as Jesus says.[7] It's like going from seeing in black and white to seeing in color, but it even goes

---

5 John 3:3.

6 John 3:5-6.

7 John 8:36.

beyond that—it's more like going from blindness to seeing in 3-D.

Do you know what a baby does to cause the natural birth? Nothing. It's out of his or her control. The decision to conceive and give birth is made by others. In the same way, the work of our becoming born again is the Holy Spirit's. The Spirit of God washes and renews us. Listen to how Paul described it: "He saved us, not because of the righteous things we had done, but because of his mercy. He washed away our sins, giving us a new birth and new life through the Holy Spirit."[8]

The work of salvation is not ours. Yes, we respond to the call of the good news in turning and following, but Jesus accomplishes the actual work necessary for salvation. The Scriptures tell us this work is done on our behalf with the eternal premeditation of God the Father.[9] And then this preplanned work is applied to us through the power of the Spirit, who wakens us, resurrects our dead hearts, cleanses our sinful senses, and seals us for salvation.

When you place your trust in Jesus Christ, the Holy Spirit has precipitated this trust in you and then proceeds to perform the divine work of applying salvation in your life.

Closer than Your Skin //

In the Old Testament days, the Spirit of God visited believers. But Jesus proposed something different—he promised a Helper who would live within his followers. So when the Spirit came upon the disciples on the Day of Pentecost, instead of performing a miraculous feat and then departing, the Spirit took up residency within each of the believers.

Paul asked the Corinthians in a letter, "Don't you realize that all of you together are the temple of God and that the Spirit of God lives in you?"[10] The word "lives" indicates permanency. The Spirit is at home in the believer. We are God's temple. At the point of salvation, the Spirit of God indwells the new follower of

---

8 *Titus 3:5.*

9 *Romans 8:29; Ephesians 1:5, 11.*

10 *1 Corinthians 3:16.*

YOU ARE SEALED UNTIL THE DAY OF REDEMPTION, SECURE IN THE HOLY SPIRIT UNTIL YOU GET TO HEAVEN.

Christ, remaining available 24/7 to help, to correct, to console, and to guide. The Holy Ghost is in the house!

Because God is omnipresent, he is still everywhere all the time, but the indwelling of the Spirit means that he is inside of you. He will never leave you nor forsake you.[11] He is always closer than your skin.

We are not talking about your conscience. Your conscience is your moral and ethical barometer, perhaps established by virtue of being created in the image of God but no doubt also programmed by how you were raised. Your conscience may or may not be an adequate guide for you,[12] but the Holy Spirit is an actual person who lives in you, and because he is the perfect and holy and all-knowing God himself, the Spirit will always guide you in the right way and never ever steer you wrong. In Romans 9:1, what Paul attributes to a good conscience he attributes to the work of the Holy Spirit keeping his conscience clear and pure.

Seal the Deal //

Does your car have an alarm system? Mine does. Sometimes I think these things were invented by the devil. I once had a rude awakening in the middle of the night when my car alarm suddenly went off. I scrambled in the dark to get my jeans on and stumbled outside to disengage the system that was intended to keep the bad guys away, not annoy my neighbors at two in the morning.

When it works the way it's designed, a security system protects its possessor from theft and fraud. In the ancient world the signet ring was the security system of the well-to-do. A king would wear a signet ring, and after writing a letter, he would seal the scroll with a drop of wax, carefully imprinting his signet in the warm wax. This sealed the message until the intended recipient could open it. It also marked the message as originating from the owner of the seal.

---

11 *Hebrews 13:5.*

12 *In 1 Timothy 4:1, Paul indicates one's conscience can be polluted by sin like skin can be marred with a hot iron, and in Titus 1:15 he reiterates that a conscience can be corrupted.*

Paul used this imagery to describe one of the actions of the Holy Spirit: "It's in Christ that you, once you heard the truth and believed it (this Message of your salvation), found yourselves home free—signed, sealed, and delivered by the Holy Spirit. This signet from God is the first installment on what's coming, a reminder that we'll get everything God has planned for us, a praising and glorious life."[13]

You are sealed until the day of redemption, secure in the Holy Spirit until you get to heaven. No one can steal away your place in the kingdom. Your salvation is protected by the Spirit of the living God.

The simple language of the signet ring gives us a storehouse of assurance. It tells us that we belong to God. In moments of temptation or trial, we are now able to remember that we have marked into us the approval and security of the nameplate saying, "Personal Property of the God of the Universe."

Fill 'Er Up //

One phrase that can cause some confusion is the "*filling* of the Spirit." Being filled with the Spirit has been associated with strange behavior and some over-the-top teachings, but it is a common phrase in the Bible used to illustrate the Spirit's control over a person in a given situation.

The Bible compares two types of filling, one from drinking alcohol and the other from the Spirit. Paul wrote, "Don't be drunk with wine, because that will ruin your life. Instead, be filled with the Holy Spirit."[14]

Most of us know what it means to be filled or controlled by alcohol, from either personally drinking too much or witnessing someone else getting smashed. Too much alcohol can make us act silly, dancing on the table at the bar or finally getting the nerve to sing some karaoke. Alcohol can even cause you to sing Barry Manilow! (Scary, I know.) The more alcohol that is consumed, the

---

13 *Ephesians 1:13*, MSG.

14 *Ephesians 5:18.*

more personal control is lost. So Paul commanded the church in Ephesus to stop their excessive drinking and to be filled instead with the Spirit of God.

The text says, "Don't be drunk with wine. . . . Be filled with the Spirit." This isn't a tentative suggestion, a mild recommendation, or a polite piece of advice. It is a command that is universal in its application to Christians. (To be clear, this not a prohibition against a glass of wine or drinking alcohol in moderation, but against the abuse of alcohol.) None of us are to get drunk; all of us are to be Spirit-filled.

Now let me get a little grammatical on you. It will help you understand what this is all about.

In Ephesians 5:18, the verb "be filled" is passive. As one translation says, "Let the Holy Spirit fill you."[15] An important condition of enjoying his fullness is yielding to him without reserve. Yet it is not totally passive any more than getting drunk is totally passive. A person gets drunk by drinking; we become filled with the Spirit by surrendering to Christ and asking to be filled. And yet when we are drunk, and when we are filled by the Spirit, we are under the control of an outside force we've let inside. Our passivity is subsumed by the control of what we've consumed. As John Stott explains, "A drunk person is under the control of alcohol, and will think, speak, and act in ways not natural when sober. [Similarly,] a Christian who is filled with the Spirit will think, speak, and act in ways not natural when he or she is controlled by the flesh. Thus a Spirit-filled life is simply a Spirit-controlled life."[16]

The command to "be filled" with the Spirit is also in the present tense. This indicates not some dramatic or decisive experience that will settle the issue for good but rather a continuous action of being filled. Although all believers are sealed by the Spirit, not all believers remain filled, for the sealing is past and finished, while the filling is (or should be) present and continuous.

When you research the many times this phrase is used in

---

15 *Ephesians 5:18, NEB.*

16 *John R. W. Stott,* Baptism and Fullness *(Downers Grove, IL: InterVarsity Press, 1964), 72.*

the Bible, you will see the Spirit filling people to teach, preach, prophesy, build, create art, dance, heal, speak in a different language, go on a mission journey, share the gospel, and so on. There are many tasks the Spirit fills a believer to accomplish.

MOST OF US GIVE THANKS
SOMETIMES FOR SOME THINGS;
SPIRIT-FILLED BELIEVERS
GIVE THANKS ALWAYS
FOR ALL THINGS. //

Internal GPS //

The important truth here is that God the Spirit can guide you from within, like an internal GPS. If you trust Christ, the Spirit lives in you. But you can refuse his help. You can send him off to a corner of your soul and live your life without his help or guidance.

What does it look like to be filled with the Spirit? Paul tells us as he outlines the effects of being Spirit-filled. Returning to Ephesians 5:18-21, we read: "Don't be drunk with wine, because that will ruin your life. Instead, be filled with the Holy Spirit, singing psalms and hymns and spiritual songs among yourselves, and making music to the Lord in your hearts. And give thanks for everything to God the Father in the name of our Lord Jesus Christ. And further, submit to one another out of reverence for Christ."

There are several evidences of the fullness of the Spirit. The first is singing. Paul said, "Sing to one another." This may sound scary for those of us who sound like *American Idol* hopeful Sanjaya or that "Chocolate Rain" guy, but it doesn't have to literally involve singing. It *can*, but it doesn't have to. It just means that our conversation is supposed to be worshipful, centered on the things of God. The Holy Spirit loves to glorify Jesus, manifesting him to his people in such a way that they delight to sing his praises.

We are also to "give thanks for everything." Most of us give thanks sometimes for some things; Spirit-filled believers give thanks always for all things. There is no time at which, and no circumstance for which, they do not give thanks.

We "submit to one another." Humble submission is such an important part of Christian behavior that the verb occurs thirty-two times in the New Testament. Not self-assertion but self-submission is the hallmark of the Spirit-filled Christian.

The results of the fullness of the Spirit are that we shall be praising Christ and thanking our Father, and we shall be speaking and submitting to one another. The Holy Spirit puts us in a right relationship with both God and people.

Gifts //

When it comes to spiritual gifts, you were not left out, overlooked, or deemed unworthy. No Christian gets coal in his or her stocking. Every single one who knows Jesus Christ possesses at least one spiritual gift. Paul wrote, "A spiritual gift is given to each of us so we can help each other."[17] He didn't say gifts are given to some, to a few, or even to the elite, but to each one of us. Nine times right after this verse, Paul used either the phrase "to one I give this" or "to another I give this," indicating the existence of different gifts and confirming the unique contributions of individual believers.

But the gifts are not for our self-improvement. The Holy Spirit who lives in each of us does give us an empowering and enabling gift for our own spiritual growth, but it is given to us mainly for the service of the body of Christ. As if to drive this focus home, Paul followed his teaching on spiritual gifts in 1 Corinthians 12 with the famous chapter on love in 1 Corinthians 13. What matters more than ministry performance is the love relationship between people.

Get involved in serving God and discover your unique giftedness, but remember that the bottom line is always about love.

---

17   *1 Corinthians 12:7.*

Just as Paul's treatise on love reminds us that godly love is not self-seeking, so Paul's instructions about our spiritual gifts are meant to help the church echo the mutual love and service of the community of persons in the Trinity. Our individual gifts, when used in concert with the gifts of other believers, build up the whole community and are used by the Spirit to craft churches into living witnesses to the amazing Giver of all good gifts.

This may be a good place to mention that some in the church have taught that the gift of speaking in tongues is the only evidence of the filling of the Spirit. There is no clear scriptural word to that effect, however. Not to mention that Jesus was filled with the Spirit, and there is no evidence that he spoke in any language other than the Hebrew and Aramaic of his place and time. We ought to be careful that we not only don't add to the word of Scripture but also don't inadvertently rule Jesus himself out of our own concept of "true" spirituality!

About speaking in tongues, the Bible *does* say, "If I could speak all the languages of earth and of angels, but didn't love others, I would only be a noisy gong or a clanging cymbal."[18] Speaking multiple languages in Paul's day allowed you many advantages. The language of the empire was Greek, but because of Israel's location, there were many languages spoken. It wasn't uncommon for people to be bilingual, but to be able to speak all of the languages that crisscrossed the Roman Empire was rare if not unknown. So if an individual had the ability to speak all of the languages of the empire and the languages of the angels, he would be pretty special, wouldn't you say? Paul could also be referring in 1 Corinthians 13:1 to the spiritual gift of tongues that involves speaking a heavenly language, a spiritual tongue not known by humans. But Paul's point really isn't about the languages themselves, but rather about the importance of love. If you can speak all of these languages but lack love, it means nothing. You sound like a noisy gong or clanging cymbal.

---

18 *1 Corinthians 13:1.*

AS THE WATERS
FILL THE SEA,
THE EARTH WILL
BE FILLED WITH AN
AWARENESS OF THE
GLORY OF THE LORD.
HABAKKUK 2:14

Spiritual gifts don't make up for a lack of love. In fact, Balaam in the Bible was given certain spiritual gifts by God, but he is nevertheless said to be a wicked person. Saul was not a good king, but he was given the gift of prophecy. Judas was sent out by Jesus to heal, cast out demons, and be used in miraculous ways. But we all know what he went on to do in selling Jesus out. Jesus even said it would be better if Judas had never been born![19]

Furthermore, Jesus said, "On judgment day many will say to me, 'Lord! Lord! We prophesied in your name and cast out demons in your name and performed many miracles in your name.' But I will reply, 'I never knew you. Get away from me, you who break God's laws.' "[20]

Love is the most important thing. More important than any spiritual gift or anything else. In fact, not having love is a sign you don't have the Spirit in your life in the first place, since love is one of the fruits the Spirit produces in a believer's life.

Spiritual and Emotional Health //

There has been a great deal of interest in spiritual gifting, but the real evidence of the Holy Spirit in the life of a believer is the existence of spiritual fruit. If believers are filled with the Spirit, the result will be seen in their quality of life. In Galatians 5:22-23 Paul wrote clearly, "The Holy Spirit produces this kind of fruit in our lives: love, joy, peace, patience, kindness, goodness, faithfulness, gentleness, and self-control. There is no law against these things!"

These are all qualities we long for. These are the healthy characteristics of a Spirit-filled life. The deposit of the Holy Spirit in us is an investment that grows with interest, like a seed that is planted and grows up into a life-giving vine. This is not some cheap, as-seen-on-TV Chia Pet life, but an abundant life teeming with fruit.

The first fruit we see in the list corresponds to our relationship with God: there is "love, joy, peace." The Holy Spirit puts

19 *Matthew 26:24.*
20 *Matthew 7:21-23.*

God's love in our hearts, freeing us to love him and love others. The Spirit puts God's joy in our souls, stirring us to awe over the incomprehensibility of grace, which in turn provokes joyful gratitude. And the Spirit, who is the Comforter promised by Christ, places God's peace in our minds. This love, joy, and peace emerge from God's perfect self, so everything the Spirit does in us and to us is conceived in love, undertaken with joy, and accomplished in peace.

The next set of fruit in Paul's list relates to our relationship with others: "patience, kindness, goodness." These traits also emanate from God's character. God is not known for sucker-punching his children, and he has no faulty temper to lose. He is exhaustively patient with us, and his lovingkindness and his goodness last forever.[21] The Spirit then replicates these virtues in us, as the fruit of being conformed to the likeness of Jesus, of being made more "godly." We learn to treat others with the enduring patience of grace because God has been patient with us. We learn to treat others kindly and with goodness because God has applied his kindness and goodness to us.

The list of spiritual fruit then touches on ourselves when it mentions "faithfulness, gentleness, and self-control." These are evidences of self-discipline brought by the Spirit's guidance, comfort, and correction. The word for "faithfulness" is usually translated "faith." But here it seems to mean, not the faith that relies on Christ or on others, but the faithfulness that invites others to rely on *us*. More simply, it is not trust but trustworthiness, the solid dependability of those who always keep their promises and finish their tasks. That is the fruit of the Spirit.

The Spirit also contributes to our spiritual health and productivity by filling in the gaps of our efforts, which are countless. The Spirit sanctified us in our salvation but also progressively sanctifies us as we continue to struggle against sin. Here's how Paul put it: "The Holy Spirit helps us in our weakness. For example, we don't know what God wants us to pray for. But the Holy Spirit

---

21 *2 Peter 3:9.*

prays for us with groanings that cannot be expressed in words."[22]

God himself is praying for us! Clearly, God's interest is that we grow in maturity and fullness in order to better reflect him and share his glory with the world. He is so passionate about this mission that his Spirit is constantly at work in us and through us to accomplish it . . . even to the point of praying *in* us *as* us *for* us. Doesn't that just blow your mind?

Pointing to Jesus //

When we are filled with God's Spirit and choose the fruit of the Spirit, we walk with God and he walks with us. As you can see, the Holy Spirit is not some religious specter that haunts church buildings. The Holy Spirit is the person of God who lives within you and wants to be an integral part of every moment of every day of your life. If you walk by the Spirit, you walk and live with God and reap the harvest of a healthy life.

How do you know how Spirit-controlled and Spirit-filled you are? In addition to the measuring stick of the fruit of the Spirit, we also measure our capital-S Spirituality by how Christ centered we are. Jesus said of the Spirit, "He will bring me glory by telling you whatever he receives from me."[23] This means that it is part of the Spirit's role—perhaps his main role—to exalt Christ in our lives and in the world. The Spirit's work in our lives makes us more and more like Christ so that we may glorify God and be ambassadors for his Son to the ends of the earth.

God's end game for the universe is that every nook and cranny be filled with acknowledgment of his glory. The prophet Habakkuk proclaimed:

> *As the waters fill the sea,*
> *the earth will be filled with an awareness*
> *of the glory of the LORD.*[24]

---

22 *1 Corinthians 6:11; 2 Thessalonians 2:13; Acts 11:18; Romans 2:4; 2 Timothy 2:25; Romans 8:26.*
23 *John 16:14.*
24 *Habakkuk 2:14.*

The amazing truth of salvation is that God begins this awareness with personal relationships with his creation. His Spirit hovered over the waters at the beginning of time. Then he walked with Adam in the garden. Then he introduced himself to Abraham and to Isaac and to Jacob and to Moses and to David and to the prophets and to John the Baptist and to Paul and to John. And he came himself in the person of Jesus and in the indwelling person of his Holy Spirit. Always loving, always pursuing relationship. And the Spirit continues this effort today, gifting us and stirring us to relate to God and to commune with God's people, all for the exaltation of Christ in our hearts and in the world, all for the glory of God in our lives and in the universe.

If you trust in Jesus, the Spirit is already at work accomplishing this incredible cosmic task in little ol' you.

Discussion Questions

1. *Read John 14:26. How has the Holy Spirit fulfilled the roles of Helper, Counselor, and Comforter in your life?*

2. *What have you done to discover your spiritual gift, or what will you do?*

3. *Read Galatians 5:16-25. What does it mean to live by the Spirit?*

4. *Which is more important: spiritual gifts or spiritual fruit? What happens when one is emphasized more than the other? How balanced are you in your perspective?*

5. *Read Galatians 5:22. List and describe each fruit of the Spirit. Pick one to focus on this week and ask God to help you develop in it through the power of his Spirit.*

HIS
WORD IS
SWEET//

✳ ✳ ✳ One of my favorite snacks is a sandwich I make with one slice of bread covered in peanut butter and honey, wrapped around half a banana. My wife thinks it's the grossest thing in the world, but I'm telling you, *it is awesome*. The honey makes it especially good.

The ancient world prized honey; it was their chief sweetener. Jewish rabbis (teachers) would sometimes take honey and put it on the fingers of their students so they could taste it and be reminded that God's words are magnificent and attractive, like honey. Here's what one psalmist declared:

> *How sweet your words taste to me;*
> > *they are sweeter than honey.*[1]

The psalmist's word for "sweet" means literally "to be smooth and pleasant." God's Word is more smooth and pleasant than honey!

Is that how the Bible strikes you? Is it like exquisite honey on your lips? Or has reading the Bible felt more like eating Brussels sprouts?

When I was growing up, my parents kept a big, white King James Bible on the coffee table in our living room. I learned to walk around that coffee table and played around it throughout my childhood. Just looking at the family Bible was intimidating. The idea of reading it was even more intimidating. I think I may have opened it twice growing up when I was really bored, and each time I could not make any sense out of it. It was like reading

---

1   Psalm 119:103.

Shakespeare or eating Brussels sprouts; I hoped I wouldn't have to do it again anytime soon.

Yet after getting over my fear and intimidation, I came to love the Bible and discovered the honey there. In one of the lowest moments of my life, I turned to the Bible and encountered these words: "This is real love—not that we loved God, but that he loved us and sent his Son as a sacrifice to take away our sins."[2] This passage reminded me that God loved me, called me, and chose me first, and out of this love I respond to him. His love is not dependent on my life; it's the other way around.

In other moments I've found hope when the Bible says, for instance, "So now there is no condemnation for those who belong to Christ Jesus."[3] I am so thankful for God's uncensored grace! At times when I've felt like a failure spiritually or blown it morally, I've returned to this passage. It reminds me that my salvation is not based on my performance but on Jesus' performance.

When I am afraid, I repeat over and over again, "Perfect love casts out fear."[4] I remember how God's love is complete and how I can rest in that love. I'm empowered to face a confrontation or an audience or an angry Christian—the angry ones are the toughest.

What Is the Bible? //

The word Bible comes from *biblios*, which means "books." In essence, the Bible is a small library of sixty-six books divided into two sections, the Old Testament with thirty-nine books and the New Testament with twenty-seven.

The Bible is like no other book on earth. It was written over a span of fourteen hundred years by forty authors from many different walks of life writing in different places at different times and

---

2   *1 John 4:10.*

3   *Romans 8:1.*

4   *1 John 4:18, NASB.*

in three different languages. Nevertheless, there is a remarkable unity to the combined content.

Although these contributors wrote the words of Scripture with their own hands, from their own experiences, and through the lenses of their own cultural contexts and personal recollections, they were all divinely inspired by the Holy Spirit to write what was written. Classic Christianity teaches that the Bible is the result of God's revelation, his disclosure of himself and his purposes to his people to be communicated throughout the world.

This understanding means that this book, while reflecting the culture and context of its human authors, transcends human wisdom and is the living Word of the living God.[5] The author of Hebrews speaks of the Bible's unique quality this way: "The word of God is alive and powerful. It is sharper than the sharpest two-edged sword, cutting between soul and spirit, between joint and marrow. It exposes our innermost thoughts and desires."[6]

God's Word is as eternal as he is: "The grass withers and the flowers fade, but the word of our God stands forever."[7] When God speaks, worlds and creatures come into existence. Planets align. Gravity submits. Storms relax. Demons flee. People come back to life. This is how powerful the words of God are, and we have this power put down in writing for us.

The Buck Stops Here //

It is this power that has led to the ideas of scriptural inerrancy (the Bible is without error), Scriptural infallibility (the Bible is 100 percent reliable in its claims and counsel), and Scriptural authority (the Bible is our correction because God is in charge). It is in reverence of our communicating God, and in submission to this powerful Word, that the Reformers affirmed *sola scriptura*. This Latin phrase means "Scripture alone," and it contends that the Bible is the chief authority over Christian faith and practice.

---

5   *Acts 7:38; 1 Peter 1:23.*

6   *Hebrews 4:12.*

7   *Isaiah 40:8.*

THE BIBLE IS RELENTLESSLY
RELEVANT AND PRACTICAL
IN ITS AUTHENTIC PORTRAYAL
OF LIFE, WITH ALL OF ITS
UPS AND DOWNS. //

What the Reformers sought to affirm—and what we must continue to uphold—is that the Bible alone, because it is God's direct and inspired word to us, should be the "decider." In essence, we should all look at our Bibles and think, *The buck stops here.* This submission to scriptural authority does not prevent people from having differing views or interpretations about what the Bible teaches, but it does at least unify us in acknowledging that our views or interpretations should be derived from and judged by the Bible and not by our own preferences or feelings. This is by virtue of the fact that the words of the Bible originated with the eternal and holy God of the universe.

Warning: TV MA //

Some people think that the Bible is an irrelevant collection of Goody Two-shoes stories. I feel like saying to them, "Have you ever *read* the Bible?" It doesn't get any more real.

In fact, some portions would be rated TV MA for violence, language, and sexual references. John Ortberg summarizes some of the messed-up families in just the first book of the Bible when he writes:

> Cain is jealous of Abel and kills him. Lamech introduces polygamy to the world. Noah—the most righteous man of his generation—gets drunk and curses his own grandson.
>
> Lot, when his home is surrounded by residents of Sodom who want to violate his visitors, offers instead that they can have sex with his daughters. Later on, his daughters get him drunk and get impregnated by him—and Lot is the most righteous man in Sodom!

Abraham plays favorites between his sons Isaac and Ishmael; they're estranged.

Isaac plays favorites between his sons Jacob and Esau; they're bitter enemies for twenty years. Jacob plays favorites between Joseph and his other eleven sons; the brothers want to kill Joseph and end up selling him into slavery.

Their marriages are disasters:

Abraham has sex with his wife's servant, then sends her and their son off to the wilderness at his wife's request. Isaac and Rebekah fight over which boy gets the blessing. Jacob marries two wives and ends up with both of their maids as his concubines as well when they get into a fertility contest.

Jacob's firstborn son, Reuben, sleeps with his father's concubine. Another son, Judah, sleeps with his daughter in law when she disguises herself as a prostitute. She does this because she is childless since her first two husbands—both sons of Judah—were so wicked that God killed them both; and Judah reneged on his obligations to her.

These people need a therapist.

These are not the Waltons. They need Dr. Phil, Dr. Laura, Dr. Spock, Dr. Seuss—they need somebody.[8]

You can turn on the TV and watch Jerry Springer or you can read the Old Testament; you'll find plenty of dysfunction in either place. Las Vegas has a reputation for being Sin City, but Vegas doesn't hold a candle to the debauchery of ancient cities like Corinth. Corinth was the place of commercialized love to the point that a prostitute anywhere in the ancient world would be called a "Corinthian girl." The Greek verb *korinthiazomai* means "to fornicate" and is a derivative of the city's name. Archaeologists have unearthed thirty-three taverns and counting so far in ancient Corinth. Jerry Springer could have set up shop there and never got canceled. There are two letters to the believers in the city of Corinth

---

8   John Ortberg, If You Want to Walk on Water, You've Got to Get Out of the Boat *(Grand Rapids, MI: Zonder-van, 2001), 218-9.*

in the New Testament—1 and 2 Corinthians—that deal with sexual conduct, relationship issues, and moral insights for life.

The Bible is relentlessly relevant and practical in its authentic portrayal of life, with all of its ups and downs. Some may think that because the Bible claims to be the Word of the heavenly God, it cannot press upon us in our flesh-and-blood, in-the-moment times and trials. But it is precisely *because* the Bible comes from the living, eternal God that it can speak to anyone anywhere at any point in history. It is relevant exactly because whatever God says is always relevant!

The Bible's hundreds of controversial topics, from religion to murder to agriculture to witchcraft, are addressed by people who lived hundreds of miles and hundreds of years apart. And yet this book maintains a harmony of values and perceptions.

It's no wonder, then, that the Bible is the most published book in the world. It continues to be the best-selling book of all time, yet it doesn't appear on the *New York Times* bestseller list. They must have felt it redundant for it to always be number one. The Bible has survived persecution, criticism, and even the natural decomposition of the scrolls it was first composed on.

In the late nineties I spent several weeks in Russia and heard many stories of the persecution believers endured in the former Soviet Union. I ate at the home of one man who had spent time in prison for his faith and had been beaten to within inches of his life on more than one occasion. As a young man, he had been given a single page of 1 John, which he memorized and kept hidden in his clothes. Tears streamed down his face as he recounted the privilege to now own a copy of the full Bible in Russian. He recalled how the Word of God had helped him pull through. He was so thankful to have a Bible that he could read. He had discovered—and experienced—its precious power. It was real to him.

Better than Wonderbread //

If we will cultivate our tastes for what the psalmist calls the Bible's honeylike sweetness, we will begin to find our reading

THE GOODNESS OF
GOD'S WORD CAN BE
TASTED, AND WE'RE
CHALLENGED TO "TASTE
AND SEE" THAT GOD
HIMSELF IS GOOD.

and studying delicious. Maybe that is a weird way for you to think about Scripture. But in addition to the psalmist calling God's words sweeter than honey, Jesus himself said we are to eat God's Word like bread. Indeed, Job said that he prized God's Word more than daily bread. Later in the book named for that man, we are told:

> *Does not the ear test words*
> *as the tongue tastes food?*

The goodness of God's Word can be tasted, and we're challenged to "taste and see" that God himself is good.[9]

Clearly we should pick up on the fact that reading and understanding the Word of God is not meant to be some dry intellectual exercise but is meant to be a savory, sumptuous experience. God's Word is the right mixture of weight and substance, more like Wonderbread to me than just any old crusty bread. (My favorite food of choice for years was a PB&J between a couple of slices of Wonderbread.)

Psalm 119, the longest psalm in the Bible, is an amazing poem dedicated almost entirely to God's Word. With the exception of just a couple verses, every verse speaks of God's Word, his revelation to people.[10] Throughout the psalm, the writer expresses the joy he finds in God's Word. He calls it the "word of truth" and in so doing makes a vitally important statement about its nature.[11] In the Hebrew language the terms "truth" and "faithfulness" share a common root that affirms that the statement, thing, or person that is true or faithful is in harmony with reality. To call God's Word "the word of truth" is to say that it can

---

9   *Matthew 4:4; Job 23:12; 12:11, NIV; Hebrews 6:5; Psalm 34:8.*

10   *In its original Hebrew, each section begins with a different letter of the Hebrew alphabet. If it were written in English, it would begin with eight lines that start with the letter A, then eight lines that all start with the letter B, then eight with the letter C, and so forth to the end of the alphabet. For Psalm 119's original hearers and readers, this structure made it a beautiful poem and one that was easier to memorize.*

11   *Psalm 119:43.*

be relied upon because, when measured by what is actually real, it corresponds exactly. We can trust it completely.

What is one of the signs you are a sold-out believer? You love the law of God. You find it liberating and exciting. You realize that God has revealed himself in a powerful, even exhilarating way. Consider Psalm 119:97:

> *Oh, how I love your instructions!*
> *I think about them all day long.*

The psalmist's excitement isn't about learning more head knowledge. It is about the joy, peace, happiness, and love that have entered his life as he studied and lived the principles of God.

The psalmist loved God's law because through it God had changed his life. The term "instructions" ("law" in some translations) is the Hebrew word *torah*. It means "teaching," "instruction," or "way." It can refer to all the writings of God in a broad sense, but specifically the Torah referred to the first five books of the Old Testament—Genesis, Exodus, Leviticus, Numbers, and Deuteronomy.

The Jews believed God had not simply revealed these words to Moses but had given Moses an actual written copy of them. (I want to know if it was signed by the author and how much I could get for it on eBay.) The Torah was the foundational educational piece for Jewish kids in ancient Israel. This was before the printing press, of course, and there may have been only one copy of the Torah in the village. It was likely kept in the synagogue in a Torah ark. They would see it only once a week when it was read from. So they would memorize huge portions of the text. In fact, by the age of ten, most Jewish boys who were studying under a teacher would have the first five books of the Bible completely memorized. By age thirteen or fourteen, the best students had large portions of the Old Testament memorized and some had memorized the entire Bible.

Honestly, it can make us feel a bit like losers. I can't name thirty-nine books, much less have thirty-nine books memorized!

But their supreme nerdtasticness should inspire us. If Jewish children with little to no access to the printed words could memorize the entire Bible, we could take a little time on a regular basis with the most widely available book in the world and read it!

The psalmist said, "I love your instructions!" He had likely spent much time memorizing it and thinking about it. He said, "I think about them all day long." That doesn't mean that he sat in a room and never did anything else. But everywhere he went, he meditated on the amazing things God had revealed.

Now let me quote you another slice of Psalm 119:

> *Your commands make me wiser than my enemies,*
> *for they are ever with me.*
> *I have more insight than all my teachers,*
> *for I meditate on your statutes.*
> *I have more understanding than the elders,*
> *for I obey your precepts.*
> *I have kept my feet from every evil path*
> *so that I might obey your word.*[12]

By meditation on God's Word, the songwriter became wiser than three groups of people. He was wiser than his *enemies*, more insightful than his *teachers*, and more understanding than the *elders*. In fact, the term translated "insight" relates to an "intelligent knowledge of the reason." A person with insight can think through some complex scenarios and act with common sense. The word also meant "to prosper and have success," because that tends to be the result of a person who is insightful.

YOU'LL FIND THAT AS YOU
READ THE BIBLE AND
MEDITATE ON IT,
THERE IS A SENSE IN WHICH
THE BIBLE WILL READ YOU. //

---

12 *Psalm 119:98-101, NIV.*

Do you want to have godly success in your life? Do you want to prosper in a spiritual sense? Meditate on the words of God! Talk about them. Wrestle with them. You'll find that as you read the Bible and meditate on it, there is a sense in which the Bible will read you. It will challenge you and change you. And as it works this change in your life, you will begin to realize how tasty God's Word really is. It will be like when a baby goes from drinking milk or formula to eating solid food. The introduction of taste makes his eyes light up, his neck straighten, his little arms wave. The rush of new deliciousness, of sensations he didn't even know existed, washes over him. And the same kind of thing will happen for you when you begin to taste and see how sweet Scripture is for daily life.

God-Breathed //

Those who wrote the books contained in the Bible were moved by God to do so. This is how Peter explained it in one of his letters: "Above all, you must realize that no prophecy in Scripture ever came from the prophet's own understanding, or from human initiative. No, those prophets were moved by the Holy Spirit, and they spoke from God."[13]

The description of being "moved by the Spirit" or "speaking from God" is what we call the inspiration of Scripture. Literally, the word *inspiration*, as applied to Scripture, means "God-breathed."

God revealed a portion of truth to the one writing. Of course, each author composed his poem or song or letter or historical record from his own personality and in his own style, but the Holy Spirit guided his heart and words, so that ultimately God was the author. God's hand was on the writers' hands as they penned their works. That explains the continuity in the collection of books.

They were all inspired by God, writing under the supernatural guidance of the Holy Spirit. As someone once said, God has spoken and the rest is commentary.

---

13 *2 Peter 1:20-21.*

Paul explained further in 2 Timothy 3:16-17: "All Scripture is God-breathed and is *useful* for teaching, rebuking, correcting and training in righteousness, so that the man of God may be thoroughly equipped for every good work."[14]

The word for "useful" can be translated "benefits" or "profitable." Paul used it once before when talking to Timothy: "Physical training is good, but training for godliness is much better, promising *benefits* in this life and in the life to come."[15] In other words, working out in the gym is a good thing, but investing time and effort into understanding the Scripture and deepening your relationship with God has both immediate and long-term advantages. Your washboard abs and twenty-four-inch pythons won't be worth much in the afterlife. That's not true of your spiritual strength.

In the 2 Timothy passage above, Paul cited four ways the Bible is valuable for spiritual training:

1. **It teaches.** You can learn so much from its truth.
2. **It rebukes.** You will feel convicted of sin and error.
3. **It corrects.** You will find ways to rebuild and improve.
4. **It trains.** You will be shaped into the person God designed you to be.

All of this is so "that the man [or woman] of God may be thoroughly equipped for every good work."[16] The result of your interaction with Scripture will be a thoroughly equipped you! Like a warrior in full armor or an athlete fully trained (or heck, a ninja, if you prefer), you will be prepared for the road ahead. The Bible is a reliable trainer and shaper of our whole selves. It is especially important to remember this in these days when the Bible's accuracy and trustworthiness are getting hammered from all sides.

---

14 *NIV.*

15 *1 Timothy 4:8.*

16 *2 Timothy 3:17, NIV.*

God Is Not Great *and* The Da Vinci Code //

One of the more recent criticisms of biblical reliability that made headlines came from *Vanity Fair* journalist Christopher Hitchens, whose book *God Is Not Great* made waves in the Christian intellectual culture even as it rallied the troops in atheist/skeptic communities. (One reason Hitchens's work caused such a stir is because he was previously considered inside the politically conservative camp, having supported the Iraq war and stated opposition to abortion. Which goes to show how much in America we have conflated political conservatism with an assumption of religious conservatism.) In the book, Hitchens takes many shots at biblical accuracy. In one particularly scathing passage, he writes that the historical record of Moses and the Israelites in the Old Testament is an "ill-carpentered fiction, bolted into place well after the nonevents that it fails to describe convincingly or even plausibly."[17]

Most of Hitchens's objections arise from his already determined stance that the miraculous cannot occur and the supernatural is just superstition. It is therefore easy to say that any document describing a miracle is "fiction." He takes a similar tack on the New Testament historical record. Tim Keller's *The Reason for God: Belief in an Age of Skepticism*, which features interactions with the claims of Christopher Hitchens, outlines a few reasons for trusting the reliability of the New Testament:

1. The timing is far too early for the Gospels to be legends.
2. The content is far too counterproductive for the Gospels to be legends.
3. The literary form of the Gospels is too detailed for them to be legends.[18]

---

17 *Christopher Hitchens,* God Is Not Great: How Religion Poisons Everything *(New York: Random House, 2007), 104.*

18 *Tim Keller,* The Reason for God: Belief in an Age of Skepticism *(New York: Dutton, 2008), 101-9.*

In addition, while it is easy to stand from our vantage point and say, "That couldn't (or didn't) happen," we forget that the books in the Bible were products of their time, impacting the times in which they were written and read and cherished, and they would not have done so if the events they purport to record were not true. The people who knew the times well would have simply said, "I was there. It didn't happen." And yet, in the New Testament days, for example, there was a tomb people could visit to see if Jesus' body was present, and plenty of Jewish men went to their deaths proclaiming the risen Messiah even though there had been no religious or cultural expectation of such a thing occurring beforehand. In other words, someone like scaredy-cat Peter would not have died for someone he knew was dead.

In any event, it is not as if claims against the Bible's accuracy are new. The charges are well worn and routine, and have been for decades. The Bible has withstood them all, both in the hearts of the faithful and in the academic texts of scholars.

Probably the most popular book in recent years to rattle those who hold to biblical reliability was not a work of scholarship at all. It was a novel by Dan Brown called *The Da Vinci Code*. (You've probably heard of it. They made a movie out of it with that Forrest Gump guy.) In one scene in *The Da Vinci Code*, a character argues that historians could "not possibly" confirm the authenticity of the Bible because "history is written by the winners."[19] Which is an odd thing to say given that the Bible's "winners" were beheaded, burned to death, crucified, or thrown to lions.[20]

Concerns or questions about the reliability of the Bible are natural, just part of being human. Certainly there will always be a need for faith in the Christian life, because there would be no need to trust God if everything we believe about him could be proven empirically through our five senses. (And even if they

---

19 Dan Brown, The Da Vinci Code *(New York: Random House, 2003), 256.*

20 *Some scholars have already done a fine job debunking the wild claims of Brown's book. See, for instance, Darrell L. Bock,* Breaking the Da Vinci Code *(Nashville: Thomas Nelson, 2006); and Erwin W. Lutzer,* The Da Vinci Deception *(Carol Stream, IL: Tyndale, 2004).*

could, we would likely just doubt our senses and the questions would remain.) But the comforting truth is that our faith is based on good reasons, good arguments, good evidence. We receive salvation through faith, but it is not an unreasonable faith, given all the evidence we've been handed for our belief, in the Bible and in the created world.

We can trust that God's Word is reliable because we can trust that God himself is reliable. And vice versa.

Getting It //

The Bible was originally written in three languages, none of them English. It was written in Hebrew, Greek, and (just in some portions) Aramaic. But while the language of the Bible, even in modern translations, can be challenging, it can be understood. You can get it. Here are some considerations to help:

1. Find the plain, literal meaning. Every statement of speech has a literal meaning. It is the common, ordinary understanding of the word or phrase. If someone says, "I was bit by a dog," you would think that a canine grabbed some part of the speaker's body with its teeth. There is no reason to think otherwise. To assume that a woman slapped the speaker instead of a dog biting him would be inconsistent with the plain interpretation of the phrase.

This is a basic rule of reading Scripture. If the passage says, "Men, love your wives," then that's exactly what it means. If the story describes fierce winds and waves breaking over a boat, then the obvious understanding is that the boat was in stormy waters.

This may seem simple, but this principle is often violated. Because the Bible is a supernatural book, some people seek to find mystical or religious meanings in everything, and they miss the common understanding of the verse.

On the other hand, when we say "literal," we don't always mean literal when it comes to poetic or symbolic passages. When Jesus, for instance, says he is the vine, he does not literally mean he is a plant.[21] But the "plain" understanding of that passage is that Jesus is using metaphorical language to say that he is *like* a vine. In that sense, the literal understanding of that verse would be that Jesus means he is a living "thing" that supplies life to branches. This leads to the next point . . .

2. Discover the context of the passage. Context is everything. That's true in everyday conversation and it's true for the Bible. If the context surrounding Jesus' words "I am the vine" situated him in a school play, portraying the part of greenery, he would mean that he was literally a vine. But that is not the context, so that is not the plain meaning.

When Jesus walked past John the Baptist, John pointed a finger at him and proclaimed, "Look! The Lamb of God!"[22] That would be an odd comment today, but the context of the statement helps us grasp the meaning. In the Jewish religious practice, a lamb was slain to bring forgiveness of sins to a person or a household. Jesus would be crucified on a cross and become the sacrificial lamb for the whole world. He is the Lamb of God! Knowing the context of the statement is necessary to its interpretation.

Context is determined by the dynamics of culture, history, geography, and the particular circumstances in which the passage exists. A prophecy written during the Babylonian captivity will be understood differently than a letter sent to a first-century church in Asia Minor. When Jesus talks to a woman who lives in the desert about living water, he is appealing to her thirst in a place where people need and want water.[23] Finding the context of a passage takes study time, but it is vital to seeing Scripture more clearly.

3. Interpret the Bible with the Bible. Along with the importance of context is the important skill of learning how to let Scripture interpret Scripture. In 1 John 4 we learn that God is love. We

---

21 *John 15:5.*

22 *John 1:29.*

23 *John 7:38.*

IF 1 JOHN 4 TELLS US GOD IS LOVE AND YET OTHER PASSAGES SHOW GOD SMITING THE HECK OUT OF SOME WICKED PERSON, WE MUST REASONABLY CONCLUDE THAT GOD DOING WHAT HE WANTS WITH HIS CREATION IS NOT A VIOLATION OF HIS LOVE NATURE.

could easily load into this information all that we think we know about love, things we learn from romance novels or chick flicks or greeting cards, but especially our own feelings and assumptions. Thanks to this practice, God's love looks a lot like the love seen in soap operas or in Barbra Streisand's songs or in the teenybopper vampires of *Twilight.* In this way, many people come away thinking that because God is love he will never allow us to be hurt (because we reason that that is not loving) or he will never send someone to hell (because we reason that if God loves the world he wouldn't do such a thing). But in these instances we have let our views of love define what God's being love means. Instead, we should look elsewhere in the Bible itself to see what love is (1 Corinthians 13 is a classic passage) and also what it shows God doing. If 1 John 4 tells us God is love and yet other passages show God smiting the heck out of some wicked person, we must reasonably conclude—thanks to the whole counsel of Scripture—that God doing what he wants with his creation is not a violation of his love nature.

When we let Scripture interpret Scripture, we begin to submit to its authority over us, and the words of God assume their necessary priority in our lives. Beyond that, they shape us, conform us more to God's design and purposes. We stop bringing our conditions and presumptions to God's Word and instead let God's Word dictate our condition and presumptions.

One person wrote these words:

> I thought that success was going to be the solution for my personal problems, but they only ached within me all the more. My marriage to my beautiful wife, Julie, had now begun to suffer and my kids were beginning to have problems. I needed something bigger than me.... That day I took a Gideon Bible from the hotel room I was staying in and began to read it. Little did I know at the time what an awesome, wonderful, and life-changing a step I had taken. The Bible came alive to me as I read it.
>
> God's Word helped me to recognize that the emptiness

and lack of peace in my life was caused by a need to know my Creator. God was not against me, as I had thought, but rather he was for me and desired to bless my life through his Son, Jesus. Soon I asked the Lord to forgive me of my sins and to come into my heart and give me a new beginning. My life has never been the same.

This individual learned that God's Word is living and active. He experienced its power to transform our lives.

You also can learn to taste the Bible as if it's sweeter than honey. You can grow to love the Word of God.

While you're at it, try a banana sandwich with peanut butter and honey. Use Wonderbread if you're feeling adventurous. You won't regret it!

Discussion Questions

1. *Why do people think the Bible is difficult to read?*

2. *What are the benefits of the Word of God? How have you experienced these benefits?*
   - *Psalm 1:1-3*
   - *Psalm 119:9-16*
   - *2 Timothy 3:16-17*

3. *Read 2 Timothy 2:15. How does a person "correctly handle" God's Word? How would you rate your handling of God's Word?*

4. *When, where, and with whom do you like to read the Bible? What helps you meditate?*

5. *Read James 1:22. Which is more important: knowing the Bible or practicing the Bible? What are you working on today?*

SAVE ME
FROM
MYSELF//

✳ ✳ ✳ **I recently had an opportunity to go back to the home in which I was raised.** My parents had moved years earlier, and the current owners were kind enough to let me do a walk-through. I stood in the bedroom that I grew up in and remembered what it once looked like. I visualized posters of Ozzy Osbourne and Twisted Sister on the wall and noted where my stereo used to sit. (It played cassette tapes. Remember those?) The room looked a lot smaller than I remembered.

The most important moment in touring my old house was looking at the floor in the center of that little room. That was where I got on my knees one night alone and asked God to help me face the addiction in my life. I asked him for power and forgiveness and grace. I confessed that I believed in Jesus and desperately needed saving. And while I didn't have a Hollywood-type spiritual experience with music and blinding light, that was where my life fundamentally changed. God met me there and answered my prayer. He saved me. Being in my childhood home was great, but standing there in that place where I surrendered my life to Christ more than twenty years ago was a powerful gift. I paused in that place and gave thanks to God for his salvation.

The idea of salvation is popular today. Bands like Carolina Liar sing, "Save me, I'm lost. . . . Save me from being confused."[1] Mickey Rourke talks about his dogs saving him. Others talk of having their life "saved" by the latest weight loss product, by the newest self-help book, by Oprah, by the presidential election— you name it. Will Ferrell, in *Talladega Nights: The Ballad of Ricky Bobby,* ran around in his underwear on the racetrack screaming for salvation: "Help me, Jesus! Help me, Jewish God! Help me,

---

1 Carolina Liar, "Show Me What I'm Looking For," Maratone AB 2008.

Allah! Aaaaahhh! Help me, Tom Cruise! Tom Cruise, use your witchcraft on me to get the fire off me!"

The Bible teaches that we need salvation, but from what? Is it salvation from being overweight or from confusion or from addiction or from being on fire? What do we need to be saved *from*? Why do we need to be rescued? And how do we know if we are saved?

What Is Salvation? //

Salvation means simply "to be rescued from injury or harm." The term can be used to describe any kind of rescue: physical, emotional, or spiritual. Yet it takes on a very specific meaning in the Bible.

On one occasion, the apostle Paul was in jail in a town called Philippi. During the night, an earthquake shook the city and the doors were opened to the jail cells. The Philippian jailer, who had been listening to Paul sing and talk all night, was certain that the prisoners had escaped. Normally he would be held responsible, since the escape occurred on his watch. He had pulled his sword and was preparing to kill himself when out of the darkness Paul and his group called out that they were still there. Full of gratitude and fear, the jailer grabbed a torch and fell before Paul. He asked, "Sirs, what must I do to be saved?" They replied, "Believe in the Lord Jesus and you will be saved, along with everyone in your household."[2]

What was the jailer asking about? Did he want to be saved from his dead-end job as a prison guard? Was he, at the same time, concerned about losing that same job due to imagined negligence? Was he concerned about the aftershocks from the earthquake? Did he eat a spoiled Twinkie? Had he heard enough of the gospel in the night to want spiritual salvation? The answer is probably, yes. He was concerned about all of the above. (Well, except for the Twinkie.) But Paul addressed only one of the issues raised, the most important one—spiritual and eternal salvation in Christ.

---

2   *Acts 16:30-31.*

The apostle invited the jailer to "believe." Then the man and his family were baptized.[3] Everyone in the household was "saved." They were spiritually rescued from God's judgment as they believed in Jesus.

Did Jesus Come to Save Us? //

It is in fashion right now for some Christians to emphasize that Jesus came primarily to teach and make the world a better place rather than to save. Jesus supposedly emphasized a political, social revolution more than "going to heaven when you die." Brian McLaren, in his book *A New Kind of Christian*, writes, "We hear 'kingdom of heaven' and we think 'kingdom of life after death.' But that's the very opposite of what Jesus is talking about. Remember—he says repeatedly, the kingdom of God, the kingdom of heaven, has arrived! It's near, here, at hand, among you! It's not just about after you die; it's about here, now, in this life!"[4]

There is some important truth to this. Certainly Jesus did say he came that we might have abundant life, and the nature of the kingdom Jesus was ushering in was real and present in his very presence.[5] But some are emphasizing the here and now to the point that the eternal stakes become obscured. This has contributed to the abandonment of the traditional Christian view of hell as eternal punishment.

This emphasis also cheapens the fullness of salvation offered through the cross of Christ. Alan Jones, for instance, calls the view that Jesus absorbed the wrath of God's punishment for our sin upon himself at the cross a "vile doctrine."[6] The trend is to create new meanings for the cross and Christ's sacrificial work. After all, the ideas of a God who hates sin and of a people who are utterly sinful make us really uncomfortable (and make it harder to sell Christianity to a more "tolerant" generation).

---

3 *Acts 16:32-34.*

4 *Brian McLaren,* A New Kind of Christian: A Tale of Two Friends on a Spiritual Journey *(San Francisco: Jossey-Bass, 2001), 107.*

5 *John 10:10; Luke 17:20-21.*

6 *Alan Jones,* Reimagining Christianity *(Hoboken, NJ: Wiley, 2005), 168.*

Christianity in these views becomes the fulfillment of life-enhancing aspirations. Or it is reduced to social activism. Here is Brian McLaren's take: "The church latched on to that old doctrine of original sin like a dog to a stick, and before you knew it, the whole gospel got twisted around it. Instead of being God's big message of saving love for the whole world, the gospel became a little bit of secret information on how to solve the pesky legal problem of original sin."[7]

Suddenly sin is not the spiritual death that contaminates us from birth like poison or cancer but some "pesky legal problem." And if you reduce the problem, the solution follows suit. You don't need eternal salvation if your condition before it is not a big deal in the first place.

Yet the Bible is clear that the problem is ultimately sin and that the solution is Jesus. After all, didn't the angel instruct Mary and Joseph to name their baby boy "Jesus, *for he will save his people from their sins*"?[8] Just sayin'.

God's Holiness, My Sin //

One still may wonder, "Why does sin necessitate salvation?" The Bible teaches that God is holy. He's the source of holiness, an absolutely perfect being without sin. God is also just. He is always right and never wrong. He does everything perfectly and he judges everything perfectly. His nature demands that he justly expose and condemn sin. He cannot allow disobedience and unrighteousness to go unpunished. That would be contrary to his holy nature.

GOD'S JUSTICE IS
THE PRACTICAL
EXPRESSION
OF HIS HOLINESS. //

---

7   Brian McLaren, The Last Word and the Word after That: A Tale of Faith, Doubt, and a New Kind of Christianity (San Francisco: Jossey-Bass, 2005), 186.

8   Matthew 1:21, emphasis added.

God's justice is the practical expression of his holiness. The consequence of our unholiness is that our sin has to be punished. And therein lies the problem, because as much as God is perfect, we are not. We need to be saved because sin separates us from God.

In Genesis we read that God gave Adam and Eve the privilege of free moral choice. They were faced with the opportunity to obey God or to disregard God's instructions. Sadly, they made the fatal mistake of disobeying God by eating from the tree of the knowledge of good and evil. They rebelled against God, and the result was the invasion of sin into paradise. Unholiness crashed into unfallen creation, and like a log of poop in the kiddie pool, it has tainted our DNA ever since.

This original event is known as the Fall, which actually sounds pretty tame, like Adam and Eve tripped over a tree root or something. But the Fall is more like the cataclysmic plunge that absolutely destroyed Adam and Eve's innocence—and consequently ours. Along with the crucifixion of Christ, this was one of the greatest catastrophes of all time. At that moment, recorded in Genesis 3, everything changed for the human race. In that instant sin entered the world.

The Bible presents Adam and Eve as flesh-and-blood people and the Fall as an actual occurrence. Our stories and fairy tales actually point to this greater reality, a first reality, that is no mere myth. In this act of disobedience, humankind fell and things spiraled out of control fast. By chapter 6 of Genesis we read of murder, jealousy, anger, and polygamy. Only a couple chapters into life, humanity is in dire straits (and I don't mean we get our money for nothin' and our chicks for free).

G. K. Chesterton commented on what happened when Adam and Eve ate from the tree:

> I will call it the Doctrine of Conditional Joy. . . . The note
> of the fairy utterance always is, "You may live in a palace
> of gold and sapphire, if you do not say the word 'cow' "; or

"You may live happily with the King's daughter, if you do not show her an onion." The vision always hangs upon a veto. All the dizzy and colossal things conceded depend upon one small thing withheld. All the wild and whirling things that are let loose depend upon one thing that is forbidden. . . . In the fairly tale an incomprehensible happiness rests upon a incomprehensible condition. A box is opened, and all evils fly out. A word is forgotten, and cities perish. A lamp is lit, and love flies away. A flower is plucked, and human lives are forfeited. An apple is eaten, and the hope of God is gone.[9]

We're not making the story of the Fall a fairy tale here, but it is part of what C. S. Lewis would call "true myth."[10] It is the true story that sets up the template for stories that come after. It isn't that the fruit eaten in the garden is fairy tale, but it foreshadows the formulas in later stories and fairy tales and is worked into the mesh of our lives and cultures.

Sin can be defined as "missing the mark." If you have ever tried your hand at archery, you know how difficult it is to hit the bull's-eye with the arrow. The flavor of this word is that not only do you miss the bull's-eye, but in fact you miss the target entirely and kill the cow in the field behind it! Sin has devastated our ability to reach out to God and to receive his favor in ourselves.

The Bible is clear about our situation after the Fall. Paul, in the New Testament book of Romans, concurs with what one Old Testament writer said in Psalm 14:

> *As the Scriptures say,*
> *"No one is righteous—*
>   *not even one.*
> *No one is truly wise;*
>   *no one is seeking God.*

---

9   *G. K. Chesterton,* Orthodoxy *(1908; reprint, Fort Collins, CO: Ignatius, 1995), 60–61.*

10 *C. S. Lewis, "Myth Became Fact," in* God in the Dock: Essays on Theology and Ethics, *ed. Walter Hooper (Grand Rapids, MI: Eerdmans, 1994), 63–67.*

All have turned away;
　　all have become useless.
No one does good,
　　not a single one."[11]

"Not even one." That's got to include you and me, don't you think?

Let's get mathematical and put this bad news together:

God is just and will punish sin. + You and I are sinners.
= We are deserving of eternal punishment.

Check out this chilling verse: "They will be punished with eternal destruction, forever separated from the Lord and from his glorious power."[12] Notice the full consequences of sin: separation from God. Sin separates people and God, incurs God's punishment, and leaves us in bondage to our desires.

But there is good news!

The Cross //

It was Madonna who ended each concert for her 2006 Confessions tour by lying on a disco cross. She said, "I believe in my heart that if Jesus were alive today he'd be doing the same thing." Um, okay. Yeah, you know Jesus, the missing Bee Gee.

What Jesus was doing on the cross was not performance art. It was a one-time rescue mission securing salvation for all who believe.

At the cross, Jesus' willing, sacrificial death accomplished a full spectrum of salvation for us, because Jesus endured that death on our behalf. Wayne Grudem summarizes the great accomplishment of the cross with four biblical terms: sacrifice,

11　*Romans 3:10-12; see Psalm 14:3.*
12　*2 Thessalonians 1:9.*

WE CANNOT FIX OUR
SITUATION AND BUY
OURSELVES OUT OF
SLAVERY. WE ARE
DEPENDENT UPON THE PRICE
BEING PAID FOR REDEMPTION
AT THE CROSS.

propitiation, reconciliation, and redemption.[13] These terms correspond to four of our needs that are met by Christ's work at the cross.

First, Jesus' death is a *sacrifice* for sin because the debt owed by our sin requires a sacrifice, in keeping with the Old Testament sacrificial system. We can't make this sacrifice ourselves because it requires a perfect sacrifice (a spotless lamb in the Old Testament). But Jesus, being God incarnate and sinless, was perfect. Jesus was even heralded at the beginning of his ministry by John the Baptist as "the Lamb of God who takes away the sin of the world."[14]

Second, Jesus' death is a *propitiation* for sin on the cross, a payment to alleviate the wrath of God. Propitiation speaks to offering payment, as in paying off a debt. We know that our sin has us way off the mark of God's standard set by his holiness. That's us missing the target and hitting the cow, remember? Well, Jesus' work is like pressing a big Rewind button, paying God to replace the cow we killed and pulling a big do-over on the shooting of the arrow, this time nailing a perfect bull's-eye as if we'd done it ourselves. Jesus' propitiation is the payment that makes up for all we have twisted with our sin. Propitiation is the payment made to cover the debt we couldn't cover on our own. We just don't have the funds.

Third, the work of Christ on the cross also creates *reconciliation* between sinners and God, bridging the separation our fallenness created. (This reconciliation was physically symbolized when, as Christ breathed his last, the veil in the temple was torn top to bottom.[15]) In the work of Christ on the cross, we are reunited with God as our Father. The atonement in this sense is an at-one-ment, making sinners "at one" with God.

Finally, Jesus' work on the cross was a work of *redemption,*

---

13 *This material and the explanations following are drawn from Wayne Grudem,* Systematic Theology *(Grand Rapids, MI: Zondervan, 1994), 579–81.*

14 *John 1:29.*

15 *Matthew 27:51.*

as it rescued us from sin and death. The concept of redemption involves a person being bought back. It implies at least three things: (1) that a person is in slavery or bondage to another master; (2) that to redeem a person out of bondage a price or ransom must be paid; and (3) that a human liaison must act to secure the redemption.

As we move into the New Testament, the language of redemption is everywhere. For instance, Paul wrote, "There is no difference, for all have sinned and fall short of the glory of God, and are justified freely by his grace through the redemption that came by Christ Jesus. God presented him as a sacrifice of atonement, through faith in his blood."[16] All of the key ingredients are in this text. First, Paul pointed out that everyone has sinned and is therefore in slavery or bondage to sin. In our own way we all failed and missed God's mark for our lives. Second, a price had to be paid to free us from the slavery to sin. Third, Jesus is both the price that was paid and the mediator between God and people. Redemption points to the sufficiency of Christ because it is through faith in "his blood" that our sins are made right. We are not the intermediary; we cannot fix our situation and buy ourselves out of slavery. We are dependent upon the price being paid for redemption at the cross.

Isaiah prophesied the horror of the cross centuries before the sacrifice of Christ:

> *He was pierced for our rebellion,*
> *crushed for our sins.*
> *He was beaten so we could be whole.*
> *He was whipped so we could be healed.*
> *All of us, like sheep, have strayed away.*
> *We have left God's paths to follow our own.*
> *Yet the LORD laid on him*
> *the sins of us all.*[17]

---

16 *Romans 3:22-25, NIV.*

17 *Isaiah 53:5-6.*

What Isaiah prophesied for us here is the gruesome extent to which Christ went in order to bring salvation to us. The cross of Christ is a glorious thing, but simultaneously it is a terrible thing. We hold to the terror of the cross and the glory of the cross. The Bible calls it the "foolishness" of the cross's message—that through the death of one man the depth of our depravity and the depth of God's love are revealed and salvation is secured.[18]

Justification by Faith //

The work of Christ on the cross justifies us before God. Paul wrote, "It is with your heart that you believe and are justified, and it is with your mouth that you confess and are saved."[19] Being "justified" means that we are declared righteous before God. The saving work of Jesus on our behalf is counted for us, is applied to us, so that before the righteous and holy judge of the universe we are now declared righteous. Because we cannot be justified by our works, we are justified by Christ's work, which we claim by our profession of faith. Simply put, if we will believe with our heart that Jesus' work is sufficient for our salvation, we will receive the justification needed to be considered eternally innocent.[20]

We're not just declared righteous (perhaps you've heard the term *justified* described as *"just as if I'd* never sinned"), but also we have Christ's righteousness imputed to us. *Imputed* is another nerdword that just means "transferred into." So being justified in Christ doesn't just mean that God declares us legally right, but we also have Christ's righteousness transferred to us. Paul wrote, "God made him who had no sin to be sin for us, so that in him we might *become* the righteousness of God."[21] We aren't just seen a certain way now; we are made a certain way.

As Jesus identified with us in dying as a human, he makes

---

18 See 1 Corinthians 1:18.

19 Romans 10:10, NIV.

20 Romans 3:28; Galatians 2:16; 3:11; 3:24; see Romans 10:9.

21 2 Corinthians 5:21, NIV, emphasis added.

it possible for *us* to be identified with *him*. When we are justified by faith, we receive the gift of Christ's righteousness. This doesn't mean we don't wrestle with sin in our body. We do. This inner dichotomy is what Martin Luther called being "simultaneously saint and sinner." So justification is not just about having Christ's efforts put in our column but also about our selves being conformed to Christ's self.

This, too, is fully the work of God. Paul placed justification within the order of God's loving salvation in Romans 8:29-30: "For those God foreknew he also predestined to be conformed to the likeness of his Son, that he might be the firstborn among many brothers. And those he predestined, he also called; those he called, he also justified; those he justified, he also glorified."[22]

Justification is big, and it is part of a vast process through which God looks outside of time before time and establishes the future intervening death of his Son as the work that accomplishes and transfers salvation to those lost and in bondage to sin. All of this work is given freely to us, in the gracious goodness of God, and is received purely through our acceptance of it in faith.

Is Jesus the Only Way to Salvation? //

It was Homer Simpson who tried cover his bases when he said, "I am gonna die! Jesus, Allah, Buddha—I love you all." This comment gets to some underlying questions: is there only one way of salvation? Do all religions teach the same thing?

On the surface, the answer seems so simple. All religions don't teach the same thing. Islam teaches devotion to Allah, and Muhammad his prophet. Judaism teaches adherence to the Torah and maintains expectation of the Messiah. Hinduism teaches polytheism (many gods). Mormonism teaches that Jesus showed up in North America at some point and chilled with the American Indians. And on it goes.

---

22 *NIV.*

JESUS' SELF-ATTESTATION IS
TOO RESTRICTIVE AN ASSERTION
TO OVERLOOK. JESUS MADE AN
EXCLUSIVE AND NARROW STATEMENT
ON SALVATION ... AND THAT'S
OKAY IF HE IS RIGHT. //

But there are many who believe all religions are merely facets of some grand, unifying spiritual truth. Oprah Winfrey said, "One of the biggest mistakes humans make is to believe that there is only one way. Actually, there are many diverse paths leading to what you call God." This sort of thinking has even infiltrated evangelical Christianity. Researchers discovered that "65% of all self-identified Christians believe eternal life can be obtained through a non-Christian belief system. Furthermore, they found that 80% of that group can 'cite an example of at least one non-Christian religion that can lead to salvation.'"[23] This means that belief in the uniqueness of Christ as the way to salvation has already begun eroding the bedrock of self-professing Christians themselves.

This is an interesting development for a variety of reasons, including the fact that Christianity is not the only religion that makes claims of exclusivity. Dr. Ravi Zacharias was born and raised in India, the last in a line of Hindu priests. After becoming a follower of Jesus, he wrote:

> One surprising illusion under which the modern critic of Christianity lives is the belief that Christianity is the only system of belief that is exclusivistic. This assumption reveals a significant ignorance of all of the major worldviews present today. In reality, every system is implicitly exclusivistic. Buddhism was born out of a repudiation of two cardinal doctrines of Hinduism. Gautama Buddha rejected the *Vedas* as the ultimate truth and denounced

---

23 Ed Stetzer, "Discussing Salvation at USA Today," *LifeWay Research Blog*, May 21, 2009, http://blogs.lifeway. com/blog/edstetzer/2009/05/discussing-salvation-at-usa-to.html.

the caste system outrightly. Sikhism, in effect, rejected both Hinduism and Buddhism. . . . Even a cursory understanding of Islam conveys its radical exclusivism. Islam is not only exclusive theologically, it is also exclusive linguistically. According to Islamic teaching, the sole, sufficient, and consummate miracle in Islam is the Koran, which is only recognizable in Arabic.[24]

But in the big postmodern soup that is religious pluralism, exclusive religious claims are considered intolerant, bigoted, narrow, arrogant, and even patriarchal. In this allegedly progressive view, shaving the uniqueness off world religions is seen as beneficial so that we can "all get along," with no regard for what offense this may cause the people of these faiths (not just Christianity) for whom the exclusiveness of their claims is at the heart of their devotion.

Logically speaking, the notion that all religions are basically the same is simply ridiculous. Poet Steve Turner cannily skewers such thinking in his satirical "Creed":

> We believe that all religions are basically the same
> at least the one that we read was.
> They all believe in love and goodness
> They only differ on matters of
> creation, sin, heaven, hell, God, and salvation.[25]

No, all religions are not the same. Simple logic tells us that if someone says Jesus is God in the flesh and another says he was just a man, they cannot both be right.

It doesn't take much research to discover that Christianity is unique. For one thing, Jesus claimed that he was the only way to the Father: "I am the way and the truth and the life. No one comes to the Father except through me." Consistent with his leader, Paul

---

24 *Ravi Zacharias,* Can Man Live without God? *(Dallas: Word, 1994), 125.*

25 *Steve Turner, "Creed," in* Up to Date *(London: Hodder & Stoughton, 1985), 138-9.*

wrote, "There is one God and one mediator between God and men, the man Christ Jesus."[26]

If these claims are not true, then the Bible and Jesus himself are mistaken or lying or crazy, all of which would disqualify Jesus from being the Savior of the world. Jesus' self-attestation is too restrictive an assertion to overlook. Jesus made an exclusive and narrow statement on salvation ... and that's okay if he is right.

Many world religions have honorable codes that focus on human well-being, love, and peace. The good works sometimes associated with these religions are often a benefit to society at large. All the great religious people of human history still stand as great religious people. All of them get a high five and a gold star. Jesus wasn't condemning their acts of goodness. He was referring to right standing with God, which is a relationship issue more than a religious issue. Jesus invites people of all faiths and cultures into a relationship with God through him.

This is an important way in which Christianity is unique—it is cross-cultural. People of all cultures and ethnicities and ways of life may be Christian. But to convert to Islam, for instance, is to convert to cultural ordinances specific to Islam. To convert to Jewish orthodox faith is to convert to cultural ordinances. There are earthly cultural behaviors and ways of life to embrace, languages that must be learned. To be Christian is to change one's behavior, of course, and to embrace the culture of the kingdom of God, but because Christianity is about (a) faith and not works, and (b) loving God and loving one's neighbor, one can be a Middle Easterner in modern-day Palestine and be a Christian the same way a Wall Street broker in Manhattan can be a Christian. Faith reaches into every culture, and love crosses them all.

Another of the uniquenesses of Christianity is the scandalous notion of grace. In every other religious system (including some that claim Christian roots, such as Mormonism and the Jehovah's Witnesses), salvation is not earned fully by Christ's

---

26 *John 14:6, NIV; 1 Timothy 2:5, NIV.*

work and dispensed by the grace of God but is instead earned in whole or in part by the works of its adherents. Simply put, only in true Christianity do we find that salvation is not earned in some part by our effort.

In Christianity, Christ did the work of redemption on the cross. In every other religious system, followers do the work through good behavior or religious devotion. Their faith, then, is ultimately in themselves! They trust and hope that they are good enough, that they have jumped through sufficient religious hoops, and that they measure up to God's entrance exam for heaven. This is not only denied by the Bible; it is called self-righteousness. The classic passage on this is found in Ephesians 2:8-9: "God saved you by his grace when you believed. And you can't take credit for this; it is a gift from God. Salvation is not a reward for the good things we have done, so none of us can boast about it."

Salvation is not a result of our effort. It is by grace through faith. Remember, grace is undeserved kindness. You and I deserve condemnation for our sin, but in Christ we will never get what we deserve. Instead we receive the gift of salvation. That kind of grace from God comes through faith in Jesus Christ.

Baptism: A Pledge of Loyalty //
We find in Scripture that baptism is included as part of the faith response of those who accept God's gift. In some sense, baptism is vitally important to one's acceptance of salvation. It pictures our repentance and identifies us with Christ. In addition, Jesus himself was baptized, and that alone should be impetus to follow suit.

Some of the most special moments I've experienced as a pastor have involved baptisms. I remember my own baptism and how important it was to me. I've been privileged to baptize dear friends and family, celebrities and homeless people. I've seen eighty year olds get baptized, watched husbands and wives be baptized together, seen teenagers lead their parents to faith and

IN CHRISTIANITY, CHRIST DID THE WORK OF REDEMPTION ON THE CROSS. IN EVERY OTHER RELIGIOUS SYSTEM, FOLLOWERS DO THE WORK THROUGH GOOD BEHAVIOR OR RELIGIOUS DEVOTION.

baptize them. Baptism speaks to the reality of the victory of Jesus in our lives.

Baptism is indicative of our salvation, part of our public profession of our faith and our announcing of our repentance from sin. But baptism is no more saving than saying a particular prayer or walking an aisle or going to church or studying our Bible or feeding the poor—all of which the Bible indicates can be good signs of our receiving salvation. Some of those things are explicit commands for the saved, but that doesn't make them saving.

Salvation is the work of God, not our work. There were times when Jesus attached baptism to the proclamation of his gospel and times when he did not. What we can say is that the Bible commands baptism. We must not underemphasize the importance of baptism in the process of becoming a sold-out follower of Jesus. Paul wrote, "We died and were buried with Christ by baptism. And just as Christ was raised from the dead by the glorious power of the Father, now we also may live new lives."[27]

When Jesus died, they placed him in a tomb, and on the third day he rose again. When we become followers of Christ, we enter into a relationship with him. We are buried with him in baptism, just as he died and was buried, and we are raised from the water just as he was raised from the dead. This illustrates our new life in Jesus.

What's the Big Deal? //

So what's the big deal with going under the water for a second and coming up? What's the big deal about baptism?

My friend Chuck is a pastor in southern California. In his congregation is a man named Jimmy from Indonesia. He was living legally in America, but his time was running out, and he was requesting asylum on the grounds of religious persecution. If he went back to Indonesia, he most certainly would suffer for being a Christian and he would be abused and persecuted. The

---

27 *Romans 6:4.*

federal courts of the United States already believed that he would be persecuted. This was not a question for them. The question they were asking was this: "Is Jimmy a genuine Christian?"

So Chuck was asked to give testimony that Jimmy is a Christian. In this setting, only the judge asks questions. He looked to Chuck and asked, "Do you know Jimmy to be a baptized believer in Jesus Christ?"

Chuck said, "Yes."

Judge: "Did you witness his baptism?"

Chuck: "No."

Judge: "Does your church accept his baptism?"

Chuck: "Yes."

Chuck had a speech ready about the character of this guy, but the judge said, "That's all I need to know." Chuck tried to tell him about how Jimmy read the Bible and prayed, but the judge just said, "No, that's all I need to know."

If Chuck had said he was not a baptized believer, he would have been deported. But the only question the federal courts ask in this setting is, "Are you a baptized believer in Jesus Christ?" They do this for two reasons. First, the federal courts of the United States, based on study and research, have it in their policy that entrance into the historic Christian faith is shown most tangibly in baptism. The second reason this question is so important is because radical Islamic fundamentalists are trying to enter America to do harm, and they will say they are Christians to get in. But . . . they will never say they are baptized. Baptism is too big a deal. They can't bear to pledge that kind of loyalty to Jesus. So the screening question for our government on whether you are a Christian or not is, "Are you a baptized believer in Jesus Christ?"

Radical Islam sees baptism as a huge deal. The U.S. government sees baptism as important. And so does Jesus. The Bible casually says that Jesus went out to the Jordan to be baptized by John the Baptist. Yet for Jesus this was a walk of about *sixty miles*. That's how important, how significant, this was to him.

THE RESULT OF SAVING FAITH
IS A NEW PERSON,
A SINNER SAVED BY GRACE
AND READY FOR A NEW
LIFE IN CHRIST. //

When we are baptized, we are in effect stating, "I've made my decision. I submit to God. I stand with Jesus Christ. From this moment on, I pledge to put him above everything else—money, achievement, family, pleasure."

After Peter spoke about Jesus in the early days of the church, the people were moved and they asked the question, "Now what do we do?" Here's how Peter responded to them: "Change your life. Turn to God and be baptized, each of you, in the name of Jesus Christ, so your sins are forgiven. Receive the gift of the Holy Spirit."[28]

Three thousand were baptized that day. They didn't have all their questions answered. They didn't have their life worked out. Most had just heard the message of Jesus *that day*, but they came to follow and be baptized. You don't get your life worked out to get baptized; you get baptized as a part of working your life out and leaning in to the power of God.

Many people wonder, "If I was baptized as a baby, should I be baptized again?" Most often I receive this question from someone who was sprinkled as a baby in the Roman Catholic Church or another church tradition. This is a very important and sacred act undertaken in good faith by many parents. It carries great meaning for many families. So when someone asks me this question, I am always thankful that their parents and family committed them to the Lord and purposefully sought to honor God through their baptism. Their parents made a declaration of their desire to see their child follow God faithfully. However, the challenge I face is that I do not see in the Bible any instance of an

---

28 *Acts 2:38, MSG.*

infant being baptized or any instruction for infants to be baptized. The Bible shows baptism as an act taken by a professing believer being immersed in water.

At the church I serve, we encourage those who were sprinkled as infants to be baptized as an adult, not to negate what their parents did, but to fulfill it. Their parents made the declaration that they would be a follower of Christ as an infant, and now as an adult they seek baptism as the full declaration that their parents' prayers and wishes have been fulfilled.

New Beginning

The result of saving faith is a new person, a sinner saved by grace and ready for a new life in Christ. You are not simply a religious form of the same person but a new creature in Christ.[29] Several results follow the experience of "being saved." These are expected changes of the new life in Christ.

1. You become a child of God. Judgment is lifted forever and is replaced by a warm and nurturing Father/child relationship. Your sins are forgiven. God's grace is greater than any sin. At the moment of salvation, grace is lavished on us. Every sin ever committed in attitude or in act is cast away and forgiven. We are "justified" before God.

2. Your eternal destiny changes. A believer has certainty about the afterlife. Heaven is the final destination of every believer. The bondage to sin is broken. A believer is still a sinner but now has the power of Christ to walk away from temptation, break habits, and renew the mind from negative and destructive thinking.

3. The Holy Spirit indwells you. At the moment of decision, the Spirit of God takes up residence in the new believer. The Christian's physical body is now a temple for the Holy Spirit. From

---

29 2 Corinthians 5:17.

within, the Spirit can seal, fill, convict, and comfort. He helps the believer grow to be like Christ. You acquire a new attitude. One of the things that will not change is the nature of life. The rain falls on the good and the bad. Cancer is found in both Christian and non-Christian. Tragedy occurs to both believer and non-believer. In fact, Jesus promises suffering to those who follow him. But what does change is your attitude. Life is now worth living in a completely different way. You have purpose. You have faith in God being there for you in any and all situations.

4. *You join a new family.* A newborn baby should never be left alone; there should be a family to take care of him or her. Now that you are a child of God, you have brothers and sisters in Christ. The family of God is called the church. It is not so much a place or a building, but rather the church is a community of people who love God and connect with one another for support and encouragement. In truth, every believer is part of the universal church. In practice, believers need to align themselves with a local church.

5. *You shoulder a new mission.* Jesus left us with a job to do. God's plan of salvation doesn't end with you. Now that we enjoy peace with God, it is our honor to influence others to the same end. Through godly example and loving conversation, we can be a witness of the good news. To use the drowning metaphor, now that we are pulled safe upon the shore, we are able to help rescue those still in the water who need to be saved by a loving God.

Discussion Questions

1. *Have you ever been rescued? What did it feel like to be safe again after the experience?*

2. *If a person is "saved" biblically, what is he or she saved from?*

3. *Read Ephesians 2:8-10 and Titus 3:5. Why is salvation considered a gift? How is it attained?*

4. *What are some of the promises linked to salvation?*
   - *Romans 5:1*
   - *Romans 5:9*
   - *2 Corinthians 5:17*

5. *Are you trying to earn salvation by your works or by trusting God's work for you in Jesus?*

CHURCH
IN THE
NO-SPIN
ZONE//

✳ ✳ ✳ What comes to mind when you hear the word church? Do you think of stained-glass windows, pristine buildings topped with steeples, or Gothic architecture? (Or maybe you picture converted industrial warehouses or storefront churches in strip malls.) Do you hear organ music, bubblegum-pop praise songs, or rock and roll? Do you smell incense or coffee or moldy carpeting? Do you see Maude Flanders from *The Simpsons* or the Church Lady from *Saturday Night Live*? Our perceptions are as varied as our experiences. When it comes to the notion of church, different pictures come to mind for each of us.

When I was growing up, my parents took me to church. Once there, I'd assure them I was heading to youth group, but then I'd slip out to the alleys around the building, smoke cigarettes, and watch people go in and out of the church doors. I wondered, *Why is church so important to them? What is at the church that they want to see?*

What I didn't realize then was that I was actually watching the church come and go. The building wasn't the church. The *people* were the church. They came to worship, serve, connect with each other, sing, give, and pray together, and then they scattered into their community and left the building behind. The church is people, not buildings!

I am a pastor. That means I live and breathe church. I no longer stand outside and watch people come and go. I have given my life to the church. I love the church. So I am excited to take a look at what exactly the church of God is and where it came from and what it should be doing today.

Called Out //

Let's start with the term *church* itself. In Greek, it is the word *ekklesia*, which means "to call out." It can be translated as "assembly" because people would be called together to assemble for a meeting or gathering.

Jesus' followers shared a radical devotion to God and one another. They shared a powerful statement that we see in Acts 4:12: "There is salvation in no one else! God has given no other name under heaven by which we must be saved." The name they were referring to belonged to Jesus, and this statement was their shared confession, the rallying cry at the center of the church.

These earliest followers had another saying that centered them: "Jesus is Lord."[1] This phrase was not as benign in the early church's culture as it tends to be in ours. "Jesus is Lord" was a radical claim with sometimes dangerous repercussions. Today we put it on bumper stickers or even billboards, but in the days of the early church, that would have been like painting a target on your back. Today a cheery "Jesus is Lord!" might get you flipped the bird, but in those days it could get you a bullet in the brain. Or an arrow, I suppose.

The early church gathered in little communities not unlike we do today, but for them, to confess Jesus as Lord was to deny that Caesar was Lord. To join the Christian church in its early days in the Roman Empire was to risk your life. Joining the church then meant joining a movement that turned the values of the Roman Empire on their head. To be in the early church was to be called out of the gathering of worldly values and sinful patterns of living and into the counter-cultural gathering of redemption and reconciliation.

While the stakes may have changed for those of us in the twenty-first century Western world (though not in other parts of the world), the calling is still the same. God has called you

---

1 *Romans 10:9.*

out of your old life and gathered you with others in Christ. You, together with all believers, are the "called out" ones. You are the *ekklesia*, the assembly, the gathering, the church.

The Conquering New Community //

The church is an *organism*. The living church of God includes all believers in Christ from all over the globe since the time of the resurrection. The New Testament describes the church as the bride of Christ, the body of Christ, and the family of God. There are truths and principles that apply across the board to the church organism. Every believer belongs to the body of Christ. We also call this body the *universal church*. It includes Christians from every walk of life and culture, within every nation and tribe, of all races and ethnicities, and in preferences of Mac or PC. The universal church crosses the borders of Christian religious traditions and denominations. Inclusion is based on a relationship with God through Christ, not on organizational preferences, worship styles or cultures, or religious affiliations. We will also look at the church as an *organization* where the universal church is lived out through local churches banded together to worship, serve, connect, and grow.

Let's take a look back to see where this idea of church began.

Jesus was a Jew and lived within the customs of Israel, adhering to the teachings of the law, but he announced that a new day was coming. Jesus forecast the new community of faith that was about to change the world. Though I am sure the disciples had no idea what was coming, Jesus envisioned a body of believers that transcended nationality, race, gender, and social status, connecting people to God and to each other by virtue of their faith in him.

On one occasion Jesus quizzed his guys about who they thought he was. After they reported the answers according to the buzz on the street, Peter answered the question this way:

"You are the Messiah, the Son of the living God."

Jesus replied, "You are blessed, Simon son of John, because my Father in heaven has revealed this to you. You did not learn this from any human being. Now I say to you that you are Peter (which means 'rock'), and upon this rock I will build my church, *and all the powers of hell will not conquer it."*[2]

The "rock" Jesus referred to is the faith statement Peter made. Jesus is the Christ, the living Son of God. Upon this belief, a group of followers would emerge. Here Jesus used the word *ekklesia* for the first time in reference to the assembly of believers that would follow his resurrection and ascension. Note that he gave a very significant promise before the church even existed: "The powers of hell will not conquer it." The church is something that God designed. It is the church of Christ. Satan will certainly attack, but he will never, ever defeat it!

After the resurrection of Christ, Jesus gave some pretty amazing instructions to his disciples. They were to launch a global-sized mission to reach the entire world with his teachings. But first they were to wait for the Holy Spirit to empower them for the task. For a long time, Jesus' followers expected he would bring a political revolution for the nation of Israel like some sort of Jewish Braveheart. But they were shortsighted. Jesus had the whole world in view. The book of Acts details, then, not the apostles kicking Roman butt and taking Roman names, but the Holy Spirit coming in a powerful way and three thousand people getting baptized in one day. The church wasn't conquering through physical force, but the force of the Spirit was awakening people to the power of God's grace.

Now think about it: sometimes people say that if a church is large it is not really biblical. Some say large churches don't really teach the Bible; they just tickle people's ears. Yet we see in the book of Acts that the very first church started out with

---

three thousand people. Later Acts 4:4 says, "Many of the people who heard their message believed it, so the number of believers now totaled about 5,000 men, not counting women and children." With five thousand males in the church plus women and children, the Jerusalem church could have equaled twenty or even twenty-five thousand believers. They met in homes for community regularly and they met at the temple to worship corporately. Sure, they didn't have a Starbucks in the atrium or a rockin' praise band, but through the power of the good news of the risen Jesus and the compelling attraction of Christian community, they gathered followers by hundreds and thousands. What we can gather from this information, at the very least, is that when it comes to critical thinking about the current state of the church, the tired debate over house churches versus megachurches is not really the issue.

What we *do* see, however, is the message of Jesus conquering the hearts and minds of those in Jerusalem and beyond through the faithful sharing of the good news by "contagious Christians."

Missional Community //

The organism of the church was born before there was any organization. You probably know that an organism is something that's alive. Your shoe is not an organism, but the fungus under your toenail is. Your car is not an organism, but your dog is. A rock is not, but a tree is. You get the idea. Likewise, a church is not something you try on, test-drive, or hide under. It is something that moves and grows and has life. A church (to bottom-line it) is not meant to be a cold and dead thing; it is a living, breathing, active community of people who love Jesus Christ and live for his purposes.

FOR MISSIONAL CHRISTIANS, THE MISSION FIELD IS OUR NEIGHBORHOOD, OUR CORNER MARKET, OUR SHOPPING MALL, OUR COMMUNITY, AND OUR CITIES AND TOWNS. //

This combination of Jesus' people and Jesus' purposes is what we may call a "missional" community. The word missional is in fashion these days, and there are just as many definitions of the word and perspectives on it as there are people involved in the so-called missional movement. For many churches, "missional" serves as just the latest label with which to seem hip or attractive to younger Christians. For some it seems growing a goatee and listening to the right music is missional. But for many others, being missional is a sincere attempt at re-embodying the message and mission of Jesus.

Simply put, being missional means being a missionary.

The evangelical church by and large has come to regard mission work as something only a select few do in select places, primarily overseas. That is what we usually think of when we think of a "mission field." But for missional Christians, the mission field is our neighborhood, our corner market, our shopping mall, our community, and our cities and towns. And being a missionary is the call for every Christian, not just those called to professional mission work in foreign cultures. In some churches, the phrase "every member a minister" is popular, and it refers to the giftedness of every believer in his or her responsibility to serve the church. The missional movement envisions an expanding of that role to something that captures the full flavor of the Great Commission: "every member a missionary."[3] And our responsibility is not merely to serve our church but to serve the people all around us—in the church and especially outside of it—by being good ambassadors of Jesus.

A missional community, then, is a local church that seeks to embody in service and sacrifice the sort of neighbor-loving ministry Jesus exemplified. The goal of a missional community is not only or primarily to get people inside the church, but to train and inspire the people of the church to share the gospel with their words and deeds outside the church walls. "Missional" implies we are on a mission; "community" implies we are on a mission together.

---

3 *Matthew 28:18-20.*

Some of this may seem to go without saying. "Isn't this just evangelism?" you might ask.

The answer is "Yes, sort of."

In previous ways of thinking, Christians did see evangelism as something done outside the church walls, but this process has come more and more to reflect a sort of spiritual salesmanship, the result of which is fairly individualistic and less mindful of the way Jesus' kingdom impacts the culture of the world. Missional Christianity, on the other hand, pictures the body of Christ doing what the physical body of Christ did when he was on earth: healing the sick, feeding the hungry, rescuing the poor, and always preaching the gospel, not just inside the temple walls, but also out in the highways and byways of towns and villages. And in doing this, we both share the reconciling work of God in the gospel of Jesus (missional) and create a vivid picture of that reconciliation to God and each other (community).

A Bride and a Body //

The New Testament describes the church as both a bride and a body. Both of these images are full of life and beauty.

1. The church is the bride of Christ. This concept of the church as the bride of God reveals both the essential beauty of the church and the steadfast faithfulness of Jesus the groom. While instructing men to love their wives, the apostle Paul made the marital analogy of Christ and the church: "Husbands, love your wives, just as Christ loved the church and gave himself up for her to make her holy, cleansing her by the washing with water through the word, and to present her to himself as a radiant church, without stain or wrinkle or any other blemish, but holy and blameless."[4]

Christ loved his bride, the church, so much that he sacrificed his life for her. As a groom preparing for the wedding day, he presents his new bride dressed in white and without any blemish. Because of the sacrifice of his own blood, the church is now holy

---

4   *Ephesians 5:25-27, NIV.*

before God, blameless and beautiful. Jesus loves his bride and does whatever it takes to take care of her and protect her life.

What would happen if you attended a wedding and insulted the bride? What if you bided your time in the reception line, only to finally approach the bride and groom and tell the new husband that you very much admire him but you think his wife is less than attractive? What do you think the groom would do? He'd probably have to explain to the rental place how he got your blood on his cummerbund.

As ridiculous as that sounds, I have met many people who say they love Jesus but think the church is ugly and not for them.

I hear people say sometimes, "I just wish I had God's heart for those who are far from him" or "I just wish I had God's heart for the poor." Those are great desires. But shouldn't we also want God's heart for the church? He passionately loves the church!

People sometimes ask, "Can you be a Christian without attending church?" The truth is that, yes, you can be a Christian and never go to church, just like you can be married and never go home. But in both cases, as someone once said, your relationship with your significant other will suffer.

If you have the heart of Jesus, you will love the church, his bride, and you will see it as beautiful.

2. The church is the body of Christ. The image of the church as a body illustrates the unity and the diversity of the community of Christ followers. It is the most simple of analogies since everyone can relate to it. Just as your own body has fingers and toes and eyeballs and a spleen, yet it all moves and works together, so the church has in it a collection of every sort of people with all kinds of gifts and contributions, yet it is united in faith.

EVERYONE IS NEEDED
AND IMPORTANT. WE RESPECT
THE DIVERSITY OF INDIVIDUALS
WHILE AT THE SAME TIME WE
PRESERVE THE UNITY OF THE FAITH. //

Paul explained in Romans 12:4-5, "Just as our bodies have many parts and each part has a special function, so it is with Christ's body. We are many parts of one body, and we all belong to each other."

The parts of the church are interdependent. We each have different strengths, different personalities, and different needs, but we work together because we are better together than we are apart. Your arm would not do so well if it were severed from your body. Your arm is distinct from your heart, but you need both to function well. So in the body of Christ, the church has no Lone Rangers. Everyone is needed and important. We respect the diversity of individuals while at the same time we preserve the unity of the faith.

Paul said it simply:

> *Christ is also the head of the church,*
> > *which is his body.*
> *He is the beginning,*
> > *supreme over all who rise from the dead.*
> *So he is the first in everything.*[5]

Once again, the body metaphor is easy to understand. You can't remove your head and still drive to work and do your job. Someone would notice. You might not have to use your brain (the existence of country music proves that), but your head has got to stay with you at all times. Your head guides the rest of the body. Not your nose or your elbow but your head. Jesus plays that role in the body. He is the one who leads the church.

God's Dream //
The Bible is the story of God's dream for community coming to fruition. He starts with Adam and Eve, and later, after their sin breaks community, he calls together a people (Israel) and

---

5 *Colossians 1:18.*

unites them as his own to enjoy each other and his fellowship. They are to shine the light of his love and goodness to the world. Then Jesus comes to redeem God's people from their sin, and he begins a new community through his death, resurrection, and ascension to heaven. The community of the church is born, a fellowship of diverse people with a common Lord and a common goal.

I believe with all my heart that the church is the world's hope. The church is God's blueprint for building his kingdom through the communication of the good news of Jesus.

Government can't change the heart. Education can't change the heart. Health care and Social Security reform won't change the heart. Oprah Winfrey can't change the heart (even if she gives it a car). Only God can change the heart. And he uses people— *the church*—to reach out and impact others. Many people are cynical and skeptical about the church. And who can deny all the scandals and hypocrisy that occur in the name of God? Our track record is abysmal. Yet for every scandal, there are many churches making a real difference and doing their best to help others and love them in the name of Jesus.

There is plenty of blame to go around for mistakes and missteps. There are lots of people we can point fingers at, and there are lots of people who love to point fingers. But critical spirits and cynicism without solutions don't help anyone. I get weary of idealistic visions of a church community so perfect and pompous that even the people describing it wouldn't fit in—they'd have too many issues! My mother always said, "The church would be a perfect place if there weren't any people in it." People—people like you and me—are the problem.

I'm reminded of something G. K. Chesterton wrote in response to a fairly ambitious London newspaper essay contest question. The proposed topic was "What is wrong with the world?" Chesterton's entry simply read:

Dear Sir,
    "What's wrong with the world?"
    I am.
    Signed,
    G. K. Chesterton[6]

Chesterton's pithy reply cuts right to the heart of hypocrisy, which is the sin we all—without exception—carry around. Often our laments over what's wrong with the church reflect our finding specks in others in spite of the planks interfering with our own vision.[7] If you find a perfect church, don't go to it—you'll mess it up.

Some think the answer to the search for an ideal church is in the size of a church—from a house church to a midsize church to a megachurch. Others think the secret is in the style of ministry, from traditional to emerging. No matter how you view it, every church community will be messy because it is filled with imperfect people imperfectly following Jesus. These people may be the problem—but they are an unavoidable ingredient to church in the first place. The church *is* people; there is no two ways about that. So to have a church is to have people, and to have people is to have sin, mistakes, problems, and questions. Yes, life is messy. Church is messy. Faith is messy. But let's get over it and get on with helping people experience God's grace.

We can do this by fulfilling God's dream for a reconciled community by granting grace to each other, despite our sins and differences. This, by the way, is not usually how the world works.

Paul described this counter-culture called the church in Galatians 3:28: "There is no longer Jew or Gentile, slave or free, male and female. For you are all one in Christ Jesus." Did you see that? Your lineage, your background, your nationality, and so on, are all important, but they are no grounds, and the church is no place,

---

6 *Cited in James V. Schall,* Schall on Chesterton: Timely Essays on Timeless Paradoxes *(Washington, DC: Catholic University of America Press, 2000), 231.*

7 *Matthew 7:3.*

A JESUS-SHAPED
COMMUNITY OF
RECONCILIATION
IS GOD'S DREAM
COME TRUE.

for prejudice toward another person. It doesn't matter if you are Mexican, African American, European, Asian, Chinese, Japanese, Australian, or don't even know where you are from. You're a Dallas Cowboys fan; you're a 49ers fan; you're a Redskins fan—we are all one in Christ. The Cubbies . . . well, I don't know about the Cubbies. But that's why God is God and I'm not. There's probably even a special dispensation for cat lovers, I don't know.

When we come to believe in Christ Jesus, we come together as a community—every age, every race, every background, every demographic imaginable—and we are one in Christ. This reconciliation is so radical and yet we miss it so much today in the twenty-first century.

Thomas Cahill, in his book *Desire of the Everlasting Hills*, states that what Paul wrote in Galatians 3:28 is the first instance in the history of world literature of an argument for the equality of all human beings.[8] Not Plato, not Aristotle, not the Greek philosophers or playwrights, none of antiquity's great thinkers or scholars, not even the masters of classical world literature innovated the idea. The equality of all humankind finds its literary genesis in Galatians 3:28.

What a great and groundbreaking basis for the new community! It was radical and revolutionary. The church is a place where it is okay to not be okay, no matter what "not okay" means. The church is a place where worldly power structures and signs of success are turned on their head and where no perfect people are allowed. We all come in with our own baggage, our own history, our own past with our own regrets and mistakes. And that is the church. Isn't that amazing? God's community ideal is a community of the broken. But despite our brokenness, God has called us together in unity.

Sometimes people look for a church that is perfect, a church where the music is the right style, the teaching is always enjoyable and not too convicting, the temperature never too hot or

---

8 *Thomas Cahill,* Desire of the Everlasting Hills: The World before and after Jesus *(New York: Anchor, 1999),* 148.

cold, and most importantly, the people are always wonderful and never disagreeable. The truth is that, just as there are no perfect families, so there are no perfect church families. But there *are* communities of believers who love and accept one another. Church families retain the idiosyncrasies of the people who make them up, but when the inevitable clashes in personalities or honest disagreements arise, in the Spirit of the living and loving God, they handle them with love and grace.

The church is a place where the social stigmas that divide us in our culture fade. It is a place where hope and healing are experienced, where grace flows freely and new life is found. And there are no requirements to get in the door of the building. After all, it is just a building. There are no requirements to search and ask questions and "journey" one's faith out by being part of the witness of the church. It's an open community made so by the open arms of Jesus on the cross and the open mouth of the empty tomb.

A Jesus-shaped community of reconciliation is God's dream come true.

Gated Communities //

If a picture of reconciliation is the ideal, why do we tend to create our own versions of gated communities in the church?

I've known churches where people snub their nose at the guy who steps outside to smoke after the morning service. One guy told me that after several judgmental looks and a few snide remarks, he took it as confirmation that he wasn't good enough for church or for God, so he left. He was driven away from God by the very people who were supposed to represent God.

One friend of mine had his marriage shattered by adultery. When he reached out to the church for help, he was told he would be welcomed back to the church *after* he reconciled with his wife and made what happened right. How does one go about doing that in isolation? Was this church from some bizarro world where everyone comes equipped with mind control? It takes two people to reconcile, after all, assuming both parties are willing. And nobody could manage this difficult work without the counsel, wisdom, and encouragement of others. This family was in crisis, and they needed help, but their church insisted they find it elsewhere.

Another lady said she was leaving the church because she didn't like the type of people who were showing up and she did not approve of the way they dressed. As she put it, "I'm scared to even sit in *my* seat at church because you never know what you might get from *those* people." I think her comment was much more offensive to Jesus than the things "those people" were doing.

Why do we do this? Why do we insist that people get "cleaned up" before they come to Jesus, as if their sin or circumstances may soil him? As if he is not the one who does the cleaning? Why would Jesus tell all the weary and heavy burdened to come to him, if he really wanted them to find relief *before* they showed up?[9]

Many churches, in an attempt to deal with this messiness head-on, have come to value a sense of *belonging* as primary. Some churches have taught (and still teach) that first you *believe*, then you *behave*, and finally you *belong*.[10] For these churches, belief in Christ is the first step in being part of a church, but you do not *really* belong until you behave. It is sort of like being initiated into the club, after which you must start earning your merit badges to win respect from the other members and get the president's attention.

I agree that you enter the universal church by placing your faith in Jesus Christ for salvation. Only those who believe in the crucified and resurrected Jesus are part of this communion. However, the local, physical community called a church is made up of broken people in many different places on their spiritual journey.

---

9 *Matthew 11:28.*

10 *See Dawn Haglund, quoted in Robert Webber,* The Younger Evangelicals: Facing the Challenges of the New World *(Grand Rapids, MI: Baker, 2002), 48. Haglund states that the older paradigm was behave, believe, and then belong. I alter this order, as belief has been more primary than behaving in my experience of modern-day evangelicalism.*

We are all human, united by our brokenness and our need for God. Many churches are more or less reversing this order out of a love for people far from God. Their philosophy is, first you belong, then you believe, and finally you behave.

I understand that purists would again point to belief as the key entry point and would argue that these churches are compromising the gospel. Some of them are, but not all of them. A missional church trying desperately to reach out to their neighbors with God's love will find that a community where people can belong is critical to their neighbors coming to faith.

And, again, I am not talking about belonging to the universal (invisible) church or even to church membership. That would require a profession of faith and, in many churches, having been baptized. But I *am* talking about belonging to the community, being a friend among friends, a beggar among other beggars who know where the bread is. I am talking about the seeking, the searching, and even the self-confessed lost nevertheless not being treated as outsiders.

Such a church will be honest and straightforward about sin and salvation through the person of Jesus. They will not water down the Bible or the teachings of Christ, but they will accommodate in every other way possible. They will love people no matter where they are. Out of that love, life change will eventually occur.

Sometimes a person belongs for months or even years before he or she believes. On any given weekend at the church I serve there are hundreds of people who would not define themselves as Christians if you asked them. I have friends who attend every weekend who are Jewish and do not yet place faith in Jesus. Some attendees are agnostic but like the music. They may represent a mix of many religions, but they sense that the place is real. They are searching. They belong first as a human being in our community, and my prayer is that one day they will believe and join the universal church of God comprised of all those who believe.

GIVING IS AN ACT OF WORSHIP
BECAUSE IT ASCRIBES TO GOD
THE STATUS OF ORIGINAL GIVER IN
OUR ACKNOWLEDGMENT THAT ALL
OUR GIFTS COME FROM HIM. //

The dynamics of the first church in Jerusalem provide a template for a healthy church today. Try to picture what it was like as you read the description of those exciting early days in Acts 2:42-47:

> *All the believers devoted themselves to the apostles' teaching, and to fellowship, and to sharing in meals (including the Lord's Supper), and to prayer.*
>
> *A deep sense of awe came over them all, and the apostles performed many miraculous signs and wonders. And all the believers met together in one place and shared everything they had. They sold their property and possessions and shared the money with those in need. They worshiped together at the Temple each day, met in homes for the Lord's Supper, and shared their meals with great joy and generosity—all the while praising God and enjoying the goodwill of all the people. And each day the Lord added to their fellowship those who were being saved.*

Does that sound like church to you? A church like that in Acts 2 is not a gated community. Or rather, it is a community where Jesus is the gate (as he said in John 10:9), and the gate is always open.

Plug In //
Did you notice from the passage in Acts 2 that the early church gathered to praise God and to pray? These gatherings often included the Communion experience, "breaking bread together" as part of their worship. The church gathers to turn its attention

Godward. It is, of course, possible to worship alone, and you should find personal time alone with God, but worship is also a shared experience in the family. In a worship gathering, you are not the audience. God is the audience! You gather with the church to honor him and express your love for him. This sort of corporate worship is done primarily through praying together, singing songs of praise together, reading Scripture together, and hearing a message from the Scriptures directed to the community by a designated teacher.

Communion is a part of this worship. Jesus initiated this experience at his last Passover meal with his disciples. He explained that the cup represented his blood and the bread represented his body. In this way he asked his disciples to always remember his blood and his body sacrificed for them. Christ died for us all, and by regularly celebrating Communion—sometimes called the Lord's Supper—we are working at never forgetting the cross of Jesus.

Giving is a part of worship as well. The early church gave of their resources to benefit the community in general and especially to help others. They offered their tithes and offerings to God with a joyful heart. Giving is an act of worship because it ascribes to God the status of original giver in our acknowledgment that all our gifts come from him and because it submits to his authority in how our gifts are used.

As you can see, worship is a major purpose of the church.

Another major purpose is our responsibility to grow.

Charge Up //

The Bible challenges us to keep growing together. Too often we come to church and we think, *I raised my hand during that prayer once upon a time. I walked the aisle and I was baptized, so I'm covered. I'm good.* As if salvation is an offer of fire insurance. You get it for the security but then you file it away, never to be exercised.

But however you began your journey into the community of

Jesus it is just the beginning. You aren't done when you sign on the dotted line.

What God wants for believers is to begin re-creating them into the people they ought to be. The problem is that too many of us as adults have come to Jesus asking for forgiveness expecting to nevertheless continue walking around like a two year-old with an attitude of "No!" to what God wants to do in our hearts and lives. We effectively say no to the transformation he wants to bring. We say no to becoming healthy and whole spiritual people. We like that Jesus took up his cross, but we don't want to take up our own.

There is a statement in recovery that goes like this: "Wherever you go, there you are." No, it wasn't written by Yoda. It means that you can't run away from the stuff inside you. You bring it with you.

Wherever we go, it's like we're towing behind us an invisible U-haul with all of our baggage. (Do you know why they call it a U-haul? Because it's still *you* hauling it.) You get to the new destination, the new house, the new relationship, and you get it all set up, but the problem is you. It's just a matter of time before the same cycle happens again unless you let God into the deeper recesses of your life and let him do the work of restoration he wants to do.

He wants to create us into the kind of people the Bible says are filled with peace, joy, kindness, goodness, self-control, and so on.[11] All of these things are supposed to be characteristics of our lives. This occurs as we devote ourselves to the apostles' teaching.

The early believers also had "fellowship." That is a word we don't use in everyday language. You don't usually go to the game to fellowship with your buddies or go to the office and fellowship with your co-workers. The Greek word is *koinonia*, which means "in common." People who have a lot in common often become friends. The word is translated "fellowship," but I like to think

---

11 *Galatians 5:22-23.*

of it as friendship. Christians are connected by faith, purpose, the Holy Spirit, and the Word of God. We have the same Father and the same faith in common. We have plenty of significant things in common that produce a deep-rooted spiritual friendship. This friendship arises from community and is why small groups are so important. In our groups we care for one another and for others.

Live Out //

Every one of us is given spiritual gifts. We are called to use these gifts to serve. Paul wrote, "These are the gifts Christ gave to the church: the apostles, the prophets, the evangelists, and the pastors and teachers. Their responsibility is to equip God's people to do his work and build up the church, the body of Christ."[12]

Service can come in many forms. Helping the homeless. Working with students. Going on a mission trip. Leading a small group. Giving a tithe. Rooting for the Detroit Lions. Ministry opportunities are endless, but people don't always feel adequate to serve. One of the reasons the church exists is to equip and train believers to do God's work on earth.

Just as there are many different people, so there are many different gifts. With our gifts we act as integral parts of the body, each contributing to the health and wholeness of the community. So some are gifted to be hands; others, ears, eyes, and legs. Some may even be knee pits or whatever that space is between the nose and the upper lip. But none of us are better or worse than another, and all of us are necessary to make the body what it is. When we do not use our gifts in service to the church and the glory of God, we commit both an act of selfishness and an act of theft in withholding something our community needs. On the other hand, when we submit our gift to the usefulness of the community and service to Christ, we paradoxically find ourselves fulfilled as God is glorified.

12 Ephesians 4:11-12.

SERVICE CAN COME
IN MANY FORMS.
HELPING THE HOMELESS.
WORKING WITH STUDENTS.
CHEERING FOR
THE DETROIT LIONS.

Pass On Your Faith //

Think about it: you are in the body of Christ because someone took the time to share with you. And like the domino effect, you at some point will share with someone else. Your sharing flows out of your excitement about Christ and into your unique opportunities with the people in your life.

The role of the church in the world is to connect the unconnected to Christ and together grow to full devotion to him. Reaching people for Christ one relationship at a time will grow a church and grow you. In the church I serve we often call this "One Life Relationships."

Everyone can influence at least one person with their life. Everybody can make a difference in somebody's life. So don't hold back.

I will always be thankful for a certain individual who had the courage to live honestly before me and share his faith with me in a convincing and contagious way. It changed my life. And it hooked me on how contagious the community of Christ can be with the love of Jesus.

Imagine what might happen in your neighborhood, community, town, or even state if your local community continued the mission of Jesus by going viral with the gospel. The church has an incredible opportunity and a God-given responsibility to reach out.

I'll never forget a woman who experienced what the church is really about. She moved to our area with her husband, and she was really struggling with the move. She had a hard time making friends and making sense of life. One day it all came to a head. She sat in the grocery story parking lot with her head down and just wept. She felt so alone. She felt like her marriage was falling apart and things weren't going well. Then some random stranger knocked on her window. She rolled it down. This person said, "Ma'am, I don't know what is wrong, but I can tell that you are hurting. You should go to this church and they will help you there." She got directions and drove from the grocery store to the church building. But what changed her life was not the building but the people inside. They led her that day into a relationship with Jesus. She was back that weekend with her husband, and as the months went on, they credited the church with turning their lives and relationships around.

That is what the church is about: helping people and loving people one person at a time. I'm so glad to be part of it.

Discussion Questions

1. *Do you remember the first time you went to church? What was the experience like?*

2. *Describe the perfect church. (Don't forget the color of the nursery!)*

3. *What is one of the most positive church experiences you have had?*

4. *Read Acts 2:42-47. What activities were present in the early church? How do you see these present in your church?*

5. *How is the church like a family? What similarities do you see in your church and your family?*

6. *What are some ways to help a new person feel at home in the family of God?*

THE EXORCIST MEETS ANGELS IN THE OUTFIELD //

✳ ✱ ✳ In the horror classic *The Exorcist,* Linda Blair turns a head as a girl possessed by the devil. The copious amounts of groundbreaking Hollywood special effects turned audiences' heads (and their stomachs as well), but it also provoked a national conversation on the existence of the spiritual world. The next decade saw countless movie copycats, plus television specials, on exorcisms. The speculation and hysteria over alleged satanic cults and those urban legendary Halloween rumors kept many on edge. Even the popular work of Christian fiction *This Present Darkness,* by Frank Peretti, crossed over into the mainstream and got people talking about the devil, spirits, and spiritual warfare.

How about you? Do you believe in demons?

In the Disney movie *Angels in the Outfield,* a struggling baseball team is helped by an angel who is visible only to a young boy. Though the team makes their best effort at playing the game, their victories really result from the aid of an invisible angel. This movie capitalized on a booming cottage industry focusing on angels. Many books have been written, by Christians and non-Christians, about angels. They've been the subject of segments on television's *Unsolved Mysteries* and *Sightings.* Another popular movie, *City of Angels,* cast Nicolas Cage as an angel slumming it on earth and falling in love with Meg Ryan. We're so enamored with angels that we put them in our romances!

What do you think? Are we entertaining angels unawares?

In the sci-fi thriller *The Matrix,* the hero confronts the staggering revelation that the humdrum everyday life of this world is just a front for reality. Everything we see, touch, hear, taste, and smell turns out to be the product of a malicious computer program fed into our brains while our bodies really lie in a vegetative comatose state. Behind the scenes of the virtual facade, in a world no one knows exists, a battle for good and evil ensues.

JUST OPEN THE PAGES OF SCRIPTURE AND YOU SEE ANGELS STICKING THEIR NOSES INTO SOME OF THE MOST UNLIKELY OF PLACES AND DOING UNEXPECTED THINGS. //

Can there be any truth to that? Do you believe that there is a spiritual world behind the veil of what we see every day?

Okay, don't freak out yet. Nobody's head is going to spin around during this chapter (I hope![1]), but we are going to talk about a very real battle that many people don't even know about. You may be convinced that the matrix of your daily reality is all there is to the world, but the Bible teaches that angels and demons do exist and that a battle rages in the spirit world. If you have created your own understanding of the devil, angels, and the spirit world from watching Hollywood's portrayal of cloud-sitting simpletons or pitchfork-toting goblins, then maybe it will be helpful to tune in to what the Bible says.

What Are Angels? //

Let's start with those cute, pudgy cherubs with wings that you have in your Precious Moments figurine collection. I hate to break it to you, but that's not what angels look like. (Feel free to submit for a refund or smash your figurines, whichever seems most appropriate.) We can probably thank Rembrandt or many of the other classical artists for turning angels into obese infants, which they likely did to capture in some way the innocence of angels.

When our culture doesn't offer us rosy-cheeked babies for our angels, we get instead the benevolent but innocuous extras

---

1   *If it does, please post a video on YouTube. That would be crazy.*

from Christmas pageants. We have created an image of angels as being beautiful women in white gowns, a glowing halo hovering over their heads. They are placed on top of Christmas trees and show up in Hallmark cards. But do angels really sit on clouds and strum harps? Do they really have to earn their wings like Clarence from *It's a Wonderful Life*? Are there teams of angels that look out for us like the one from the popular 90s TV show *Touched by an Angel*?

The Bible teaches the following:

1. *Angels are created beings.* They are not eternal or almighty like God. They have not existed as long as he has, but rather they were made by him. They neither die nor reproduce. They are strong and fast, able to fight or worship or deliver a message at God's command.

Just open the pages of Scripture and you see them sticking their noses into some of the most unlikely of places and doing unexpected things. They appear in the Bible more than three hundred times. They are climbing ladders and wrestling people and taming lions and lifting weights and rescuing captives and comforting the frightened and fighting battles and recruiting strangers and giving warnings. In fact, the word *angel* literally means "messenger." Many times in the Bible angels are seen delivering a message to humans.

Daniel was visited by an angel and given a forecast of the future of Israel. Listen to Daniel's description of the one who visited him in Daniel 10:5-6: "I looked up and saw a man dressed in linen clothing, with a belt of pure gold around his waist. His body looked like a precious gem. His face flashed like lightning, and his eyes flamed like torches. His arms and feet shone like polished bronze, and his voice roared like a vast multitude of people."

Does that sound like a "precious moment" to you? Hardly a cute little cherub, is he? You can understand why the first thing angels usually say is "Don't be afraid." If they looked like Clarence or some drooling baby, they wouldn't have to say that. But if some dude showed up with fire in his eyes and lightning shooting out of his face, I would probably shake in my shoes.

Other famous messages delivered by angels include the announcement by the angel Gabriel to the young virgin Mary in Nazareth. His message was the surprising announcement that she was going to have a child. The announcement of the angels to the Bethlehem shepherds about the birth of the Christ child is another famous angel encounter. Angels also gave the prophecies of future events to the apostle John on the island of Patmos that eventually became our New Testament book of Revelation.

Probably the most significant angel message ever is the one described in Matthew 28:2-6. Some women came to see where Jesus was buried in the tomb, and this is what happened:

> Suddenly there was a great earthquake! For an angel of the Lord came down from heaven, rolled aside the stone, and sat on it. His face shone like lightning, and his clothing was as white as snow. The guards shook with fear when they saw him, and they fell into a dead faint.
>
> Then the angel spoke to the women. "Don't be afraid!" he said. "I know you are looking for Jesus, who was crucified. He isn't here! He is risen from the dead, just as he said would happen. Come, see where his body was lying."

That was the most important announcement ever made!

2. Angels are servants. The author of Hebrews asked, "Are not all angels ministering spirits sent to serve those who will inherit salvation?"[2] The answer is yes. God can send angels to do battle for us or to take care of us. This is where the idea of guardian angels originated. I'm not convinced that you have one personal angel assigned to you who will push you out of the way of an oncoming car. Nor will they magically hide the ice cream when

---

2 Hebrews 1:14, *NIV*.

YOU DON'T ATTRACT
ANGELS WITH THE
SPIRITUAL EQUIVALENT
OF BIRD FEEDERS;
YOU PRAY TO THE GOD WHO
IS IN CHARGE OF ANGELS.

you are on a diet. But the Bible is clear that angels watch over us. Psalm 91:11 promises:

> *He will order his angels*
> *to protect you wherever you go.*

There are plenty of examples in Scripture of angels lending a helping hand. Who doesn't remember Daniel in the lion's den? After spending the night shut in a den of hungry lions, Daniel shouted out the next morning, "My God sent his angel to shut the lions' mouths so that they would not hurt me."[3]

Angels may help, but remember that God sends the angels. We are not called to pray to or worship angels. We are to worship God. We don't need to be concerned about connecting with angels but rather with connecting with God.

In the book *Angels on Assignment*, Roland Buck claims that you can get in touch with your angel by color-coordinating your wardrobe. Guardian angels allegedly like rose or soft green; healing angels like deep sapphire blue; seraphim angels like crimson red; cherubim angels like blue; the archangel Michael likes deep green and vivid blue; and Gabriel is attracted to tans, browns, and dark green.[4] (No angel likes puce, I guess because puce just sounds too much like puke.)

Now, I know that you may be worried right now, thinking, Man, what if I'm sick and need angelic help, but I hate to wear sapphire blue! How will I ever connect with my angel?[5] Suddenly, spiritual warfare is like a hypercritical episode of the reality show *What Not to Wear*. But none of this kind of teaching is found in the Bible. God is the one who is worshiped and who sends the angels and gets the praise. You don't attract angels with the spiritual equivalent of bird feeders; you pray to the God who is in charge of angels.

Angels are also sent by God to punish his enemies. Second

---

3 *Daniel 6:22.*

4 *Roland Buck,* Angels on Assignment *(New Kensington, PA: Whitaker, 2005).*

5 *Thanks to Mike Breaux for this.*

Kings 19 speaks of an angel of the Lord putting to death 185,000 men in the Assyrian army. Angels punish God's enemies and they protect God's people.

You just never know when an angel might show up. In fact, Hebrews 13:2 reminds us, "Don't forget to show hospitality to strangers, for some who have done this have entertained angels without realizing it!" *Hmm.* Is there a new person visiting your small group this session? Better treat him well! (Or at least wear some soft green.)

Not all angels are so helpful, however. When God created angels, he gave them the ability to choose. Like humans, they could choose to obey God or not. Unlike humans, though, if angels rebel against God, there is no redemption for them. One angel rebelled, and when he did, he took other angels with him.

Who Is Satan? //

Consider the story of Reagan, the twelve-year-old daughter of Chris McNeal. A shaking bed, along with odd noises, were the first signs that something was happening in Reagan's bedroom. As time wore on, little Reagan became the victim of physical and mental disorders that were beyond medical explanation. Completely frustrated, her mother was forced to consider the possibility that evil spirits had taken control of her daughter's body. Chris McNeal, who had denied the existence of God plenty of times, thought it all seemed incredible, but she had tried everything else and she was at the end of her rope. So she turned to two Catholic priests who agreed to perform exorcism rites. The grotesque description of the events that followed included the horrifying contortions of Reagan's body during the ritual. All of this was part of the highly acclaimed book *The Exorcist* and the film that came from the book.

What do you believe about the devil? A recent survey of American religious beliefs conducted by the Barna Group reveals that only 27 percent of American adults agree that Satan is a real force. Another survey, this time of Christians, revealed that 40 percent of believers in Christ agree with the statement that Satan "is not a living being but is a symbol of evil."[6]

The Bible would beg to differ. The Bible teaches that Satan was originally created by God like all other angels, but it wasn't enough for him. In Ezekiel we find a description of the devil before he rebelled. He was beautiful.

> *You were the model of perfection,*
>> *full of wisdom and perfect in beauty. . . .*
> *You were anointed as a guardian cherub,*
>> *for so I ordained you.*
> *You were on the holy mount of God;*
>> *you walked among the fiery stones.*
> *You were blameless in your ways*
>> *from the day you were created*
>> *till wickedness was found in you. . . .*
> *Your heart became proud*
>> *on account of your beauty,*
> *and you corrupted your wisdom*
>> *because of your splendor.*
> *So I threw you to the earth.*[7]

So Satan was cast out of heaven, taking with him a contingent of the heavenly host. Revelation 12:7-9 depicts the very first spiritual war: "Then there was war in heaven. Michael and his angels fought against the dragon and his angels. And the dragon lost the battle, and he and his angels were forced out of heaven. This great dragon—the ancient serpent called the devil, or Satan, the one deceiving the whole world—was thrown down to the earth with all his angels."

6   Barna Group, "Barna Survey Examines Changes in Worldview Among Christians over the Past 13 Years," http://www.barna.org/barna-update/article/21-transformation/252-barna-survey-examines-changes-in-worldview-among-christians-over-the-past-13-years; Barna Group, "Most American Christians Do Not Believe That Satan or the Holy Spirit Exist," http://www.barna.org/barna-update/article/12-faithspirituality/260-most-american-christians-do-not-believe-that-satan-or-the-holy-spirit-exis.

7   Ezekiel 28:12, 14-15, 17, NIV.

A SPIRITUAL BATTLE
IS BEING WAGED,
AND WE MUST
BE READY. //

We next see the devil in the form of a serpent in the Garden of Eden. It was the serpent that tempted Eve to disobey God and in so doing precipitated the human race's fall into sin. He was literally hell-bent on destroying the work of God by any means he could.

The devil is called Satan, Lucifer, Beelzebub, the dragon, the prince of darkness, and the god of this world. He represents everything evil. But do not be naive. He won't show up with a pitchfork in hand. The Bible says in 2 Corinthians 11:14 that "Satan . . . masquerades as an angel of light."[8]

Remember that hit song from Terri Gibbs?

> Somebody's knocking, should I let him in?
> Lord, it's the devil, would you look at him?
> I've heard about him, but I never dreamed
> He'd have blue eyes and blue jeans.

Okay, if you weren't around in the early 80s, you probably don't remember it, but Terri did a good job of casting the devil in the guise of a tempting lover. This was fitting, because Satan masquerades as an angel of light. He is the father of lies, the tempter, and the accuser of the saints.

Satan met Jesus in the wilderness to attempt to corrupt his life and ministry. He entered the heart of Judas to betray Jesus and send him to the cross. He unleashed a host of demons (fallen angels) on this world who infiltrate weak lives and weak minds. He plans on ruling the world someday with the emergence of an Antichrist, whom he will control. All this shows he is not one to take lightly.

---

8 *NIV.*

GOOD SPIRITUAL WARRIORS
DON'T DENY THE BATTLE,
BUT NEITHER DO THEY
ATTACK EVERY TOWN THEY
ENTER. GOOD WARRIORS
ARE ON THE ALERT AND
AWARE OF THE ENEMY.

But he will ultimately be cast into the lake of fire at the end of the age. In other words, as powerful and scary as the devil might be, his destiny is already determined. It's probably one of the things that inflames him so much and why he so ruthlessly opposes God.

Not all sin and evil can be blamed on the devil, however. The old phrase "The devil made me do it!" doesn't always wash. We are perfectly capable of causing plenty of trouble without the enemy's help. But the devil and his minions are always on the prowl to distort the truth about God and to keep the world blinded to the gospel. Second Corinthians 4:4 says, "Satan, who is the god of this world, has blinded the minds of those who don't believe. They are unable to see the glorious light of the Good News." I believe that behind social vices like drugs, pornography, crime, and corruption are the influences of the demonic world, angels who hinder rather than help the purposes of God. (I wouldn't be surprised if they were the masterminds behind telemarketing also.)

If we had eyes that could see the spirit world, we would be shocked at what is going on around us. The servant of the prophet Elisha was given the unique privilege of seeing behind the scenes. The city was surrounded with military troops ready to capture his friend, Elisha. Then look what happened:

> When the servant of the man of God got up early the next morning and went outside, there were troops, horses, and chariots everywhere. "Oh, sir, what will we do now?" the young man cried to Elisha.
>
> "Don't be afraid!" Elisha told him. "For there are more on our side than on theirs!" Then Elisha prayed, "O LORD, open his eyes and let him see!" The LORD opened the young man's eyes, and when he looked up, he saw that the hillside around Elisha was filled with horses and chariots of fire.[9]

---

9   2 Kings 6:15-17.

Wow! God's armies are ready for battle. Wouldn't you love to be able to see them like that?

Paul warned us that our fight is not against the people of this world: "We are not fighting against flesh-and-blood enemies, but against evil rulers and authorities of the unseen world, against mighty powers in this dark world, and against evil spirits in the heavenly places."[10] That means that we need to be aware of what is happening behind the scenes in the spirit world.

Spiritual Warfare //

A spiritual battle is being waged, and we must be ready. I'm not talking about sprinkling holy water on undead hordes or warding off demons with a crucifix (although that does sound pretty cool). You don't have to school yourself in Krav Maga and become Buffy the Vampire Slayer. I am referring to doing spiritual battle against the forces of evil with a strong, prayerful, righteous lifestyle.

Jesus dealt with demonic possession in his ministry. One man he encountered gave his name as Legion because he was possessed by so many demons. Jesus cast the demons into a herd of pigs (and thereby invented deviled ham).

Seriously, though, it is very possible for a person to be inhabited by demons. I once had breakfast with an intelligent theologian, one who easily earned the respect of his academic and pastoral peers. This guy wasn't a wacko. He said he'd personally documented hundreds of accounts of demon possession around the world. Yet he believed that demons can only oppress Christians, but not possess us, because he who is in us (the Holy Spirit of God) is greater than he who is in the world (the devil)."[11]

Yet demonic possession may not be the most effective way for the devil to influence society, and exorcism will probably not be the primary type of spiritual warfare you will engage in.

---

10 *Ephesians 6:12.*

11 *1 John 4:4.*

I'm not recommending you turn into Scooby-Doo or a ghost-buster, but here are some biblical guidelines for combating your enemy.

A BELIEVER WHO
IS IGNORANT OF
SATAN'S SCHEMES WILL BE
EASILY DEFEATED. //

1. Be aware. Christians can run to one of two extremes when it comes to the spirit world: complete ignorance or overzealous demonizing. In the introduction to his classic work of creative devilry, C. S. Lewis identifies the two opposing errors when it comes to the subject of demons: "One is to disbelieve in their existence. The other is to believe, and to feel an excessive and unhealthy interest in them. They themselves are equally pleased by both errors and hail a materialist or a magician with the same delight."[12]

Some people refuse to believe in angels and demons. They view them as mythological beings not worthy of the attention of intelligent twenty-first-century minds. Unfortunately, that's exactly where the devil wants them. A believer who is ignorant of Satan's schemes will be easily defeated. On the other hand, the overzealous Christian will find a demon under every bush. This kind of person will try to cast out the demons of procrastination or car trouble, burn the latest Harry Potter book, and boycott *Bewitched* reruns.

Good spiritual warriors don't deny the battle, but neither do they attack every town they enter. Good warriors are on the alert and aware of the enemy. Therefore, Peter warned, "Stay alert! Watch out for your great enemy, the devil. He prowls around like a roaring lion, looking for someone to devour."[13]

An effective way of being alert is to ask every now and then, "If I were the enemy, where would I attack?" Have you ever

---

12 *C. S. Lewis,* The Screwtape Letters *(New York: Macmillan, 1943), 9.*

13 *1 Peter 5:8.*

noticed that just before you head off to small group or to church or to be involved in a ministry, something goes awry? Friction stirs in your relationships or circumstances get busy or you are tempted not to go. Don't be naive. Someone is working against you! Be aware . . . be very aware, but . . .

2. Don't be afraid. Yes, the devil has supernatural power that you don't have, but God is way more powerful than Satan, and he has given you authority over demons.[14] Remember, God is the almighty ruler of the universe, and the devil is only one created being. God is all knowing, all powerful, and always present. Satan is not. That's why this promise is so reassuring: "You belong to God, my dear children. You have already won a victory over those people, because the Spirit who lives in you is greater than the spirit who lives in the world."[15] The Holy Spirit who dwells within the believer is far greater than the evil spirits of this world. Fear and lies are the devil's greatest weapons. If you refuse to fear him or to believe him, you will defeat him.

3. Resist the devil. "Resisting," in this instance, means standing up against something. If you have ever tried to feed vegetables to a one-year-old, you have experienced resistance. Thrashing arms and clenched jaws cannot be overcome by a spoonful of spinach. In similar fashion, even the weakest believer indwelled by the Spirit can exert authority in resistance of Satan, because the work of resistance is assured by the power of Christ on the cross. The devil will always attack, but you can resist him. James wrote, "Resist the devil, and he will flee from you."[16]

You are a child of God, so stand your ground.

The Bible says Satan is the father of lies.[17] He whispers to you, "If God were really powerful, he would have answered that prayer

---

14 Luke 10:18-20.

15 1 John 4:4.

16 James 4:7.

17 John 8:44.

you have been praying. But he is not powerful. He is weak." He says, "If God were really present, you would feel his presence. But you don't and that's because he doesn't exist." He says, "Do you think for one moment that he is going to forgive that sin, again and again?"

You see, he whispers these lies about God to us in hopes that we will believe them and as a result will withdraw from God, the source of light. Satan tries to deceive us about sin, about the consequences of it. He whispers, "You deserve a break. It's only one harmless thing; it's not going to hurt anybody. Besides, you work so hard; you are so faithful; you are so good all the time. You can afford a little fun. Go ahead."

Satan tells us common lies like these: we deserve things we don't; nobody will find out the things we do; that sin won't hurt anybody. But you can resist him by surrendering to God. You trust God's Word over Satan's lies. You put your faith in God! Doing so is like punching Satan in the throat.

Eve failed this test when the serpent started twisting God's words in his temptation. She was able to correct Satan at first with what God had really said, but then her memory of (or commitment to) God's words failed and she couldn't counter Satan's lies with Scripture. But when Satan tempted Jesus in the desert, Jesus did not run out of Scripture. He countered every one of Satan's perversions of Scripture with firm declarations of biblical wisdom.[18] Learn this lesson well: don't run out of Scripture!

*4. **Live wisely.*** Idle hands may or may not be the devil's playground, but unconfessed sin always will be. Persistent disobedience in your life will provide your enemy with a platform to build a bunker. It is a strategic opportunity for him. When you ignore God's wisdom and guidance, instead of resisting the enemy, you allow him a place to invade your world.

---

18 *See Matthew 4.*

YOU STAND FIRM BY GETTING ON
YOUR KNEES. NO OTHER ARMY ON EARTH
DROPS TO THEIR KNEES TO ENGAGE
THE ENEMY EXCEPT THE
FOLLOWERS OF JESUS. //

Paul told us simply, "Do not give the devil a foothold."[19] A foothold is a place where the devil can find sure footing and hang on. The context of this statement by Paul is a laundry list of destructive behaviors, including theft, abuse, violence, dishonesty, bitterness, and slander. These attitudes and activities open the door for the enemy, so confess them as sin and ask God to help you live wisely.

5. *Wear your armor.* If you were going onto the football field, you would want to be dressed in full protective gear: shoes, kneepads, shoulder pads, and especially a helmet. You wouldn't want to play against the other team in pajamas or a Speedo. (Actually, dudes, unless you're a professional swimmer, there are no circumstances acceptable for you to wear a Speedo.) Any warrior knows that you need to be dressed for battle if you are going to realize victory. What's true of action on the playing field and the battlefield is true for waging war on the spiritual plane. You need spiritual weaponry to battle the spirit world.

The most famous passage on spiritual warfare is found in the letter to the Ephesians. The apostle Paul was a veteran soldier in spiritual battle and he gave seasoned advice for all who encounter the forces of darkness: "Be strong in the Lord and in his mighty power. Put on all of God's armor so that you will be able to stand firm against all strategies of the devil."[20]

Note three things right off the bat. First, you have to dress yourself. These pieces of spiritual weaponry are not automatically with you as a Christ follower. This is the real world. Every

---

19 *Ephesians 4:27, NIV.*
20 *Ephesians 6:10-11.*

day, you need to make the effort to get dressed. Second, you need to put on all of it. The "full" armor means every piece of it. No matter how good your shoulder pads are, for example, you still need your helmet. Third, it is the armor of God. This weaponry is not of your own making. This armor is not something you can fabricate or learn from Dr. Phil. It is spiritual in nature and comes from God.

Paul described the armor for spiritual warfare by recalling the image of a Roman soldier commonly seen in the first-century world. He named four pieces of protective armor and two offensive weapons. In Ephesians 6:14-18 we read:

> *Stand your ground, putting on the belt of truth and the body armor of God's righteousness. For shoes, put on the peace that comes from the Good News so that you will be fully prepared. In addition to all of these, hold up the shield of faith to stop the fiery arrows of the devil. Put on salvation as your helmet, and take the sword of the Spirit, which is the word of God.*
>
> *Pray in the Spirit at all times and on every occasion. Stay alert and be persistent in your prayers for all believers everywhere.*

If you are dressed for battle with truth, righteousness, the gospel, faith, salvation, and the Word of God, the enemy is no match for you.

Paul also talked about prayer. It may sound strange, but you stand firm by getting on your knees. No other army on earth drops to their knees to engage the enemy except the followers of Jesus.

Nearer than You Think //

Billy Graham wrote in his book *Angels: God's Secret Agents* about a missionary named John Payton. Hostile natives surrounded his missionary village, intent on burning out the village and killing all the people who lived there. The Paytons prayed all night long that those hostile tribesmen would not burn down the village and destroy them. The next morning, they arose to find that all the aggressors had gone.

About three months later, the chief of those same hostile tribesmen became a Christian. Payton asked him about that terrible night: "When you and your tribesmen had surrounded our village, why didn't you come in and kill us?"

The chief responded, "We couldn't. We weren't about to fight all those men."

Payton asked, "What men?"

The chief said, "All those huge, dazzling, bright men with their swords drawn. We knew we would be killed if we tried to attack them."

Then Billy Graham writes, "Believers, look up—take courage. The angels are nearer than you think."[21]

Have faith, be encouraged, and remember: he who is in you is greater than he who is in the world.

---

21 *Billy Graham,* Angels: God's Secret Agents *(Nashville: Thomas Nelson, 1995), 39.*

Discussion Questions

1. *What are some common perceptions about angels and demons?*

2. *Read Luke 15:10, 1 Corinthians 4:9, and 1 Peter 1:12. What do angels watch instead of TV?*

3. *What kind of spiritual warfare are you experiencing?*

4. *If you were the enemy, how would you attack your life or your church today? How can you be ready for his attacks?*

5. *Do you suspect that you have been visited by an angel? Do tell.*

6. *Read Ephesians 6:10-18. Identify each piece of armor. How are you dressed for battle?*

RETURN
OF THE
KING//

✳ ✳ ✳ H. G. Wells wrote his famous novel *The Time Machine* in 1895. In this piece of science fiction, a time traveler builds a machine that can journey into the future. As he experiments with his invention, he discovers that the world as he knows it becomes a place of slavery and rampant abuse. Entire cities and cultures have devolved into chaos, with wars upon wars. Eventually the human race is nearly unrecognizable, living in an uncultivated jungle with no discernible community or language, fearing for their lives from mutant creatures who rule the earth from hellish caverns below the surface. They didn't even have those cool hoverboards like in *Back to the Future Part II*.

Fortunately, *The Time Machine*—and works following in its footsteps, such as *The Road Warrior* movies—are just fiction.

Another great story, with an apocalypse too great for even the biggest Hollywood budgets, reveals a picture of the future that includes both trouble *and* utopia. And this is no fiction. What is this story? You guessed it: it's the story we find in the Bible.

Before Ahnuld the Terminator made famous the words "I'll be back!," Jesus made a promise to his followers that he would return to earth someday. For the last two thousand years, Christians have lived in the hope of his coming. This hopeful thinking of the "last things" is what is called *eschatology*, the study of the end times.

Common Grounds //

Let me caution you. This is one of the most fascinating areas of Bible teaching but also one of the most problematic. It is an area where really smart people have differing views. And where really, um, "interesting" people have far-out views. But there are a few things nearly all those who study the end times can agree on.

1. No one knows exactly when Jesus will return. Jesus spoke often about his return, but he never revealed the actual date and time. Jesus said, "No one knows the day or hour when these things will happen, not even the angels in heaven or the Son himself. Only the Father knows."[1]

Yet people continue to disregard Jesus' teaching and try to predict his return. One author forewarned, "Desolating earthquakes, sweeping fires, distressing poverty, political profligacy, private bankruptcy and widespread immorality which abound in these last days, obviously indicate that the Lord is returning immediately." These words were written by William Miller in 1843. On October 22, 1844, Miller took thousands of followers to a mountain and they waited all night for Jesus to return. They sold their property, threw everything to the wind, and headed for the mountains. Some climbed trees and watched the stars and waited. On the morning of October 23, after nothing happened, they walked back into the city amid jeering and taunting. It was a tragic day in church history.[2]

Then there is Edgar Whisenant. After September 1, 1989, Whisenant said to the press, "I can stand in front of the Lord and say I gave it my best shot." Was Whisenant trying out for the Olympic team or something? No, he was wrapping up several years of the equally Herculean effort of mathematical gymnastics and biblical contortionism required in predicting the date of Jesus' return. Whisenant wrote a book in the mid-1980s titled *88 Reasons Why the Rapture Will Happen in 1988.* He reasoned this way: We can't know the day or the hour, but we can know the month and the year. Pretty clever, eh?

---

1 *Matthew 24:36.*

2 *Robert G. Clouse, Robert N. Hosack, and Richard V. Pierard,* The New Millennium Manual *(Grand Rapids, MI: BridgePoint, 1999), 112–15.*

GOD WANTS US TO TRUST IN HIS
SOVEREIGN CONTROL OF THE UNIVERSE
AND TO LOOK FORWARD TO THE
DAY OF REWARD THAT
AWAITS HIS FOLLOWERS. //

When the Rapture failed to obey Whisenant's forecast in 1988, he didn't close up shop and apologize but instead produced a sequel on why the Rapture would happen in 1989. (He'd apparently forgotten to carry the 2 in some formula involving biblical generations, planetary orbits, and the number of variations of Coca-Cola on the market.) After a 0 for 2 record in predicting when Jesus will return, the retired NASA engineer, who lived in a one-room shack outside Little Rock, Arkansas, said his job was done. His book predicting the 1989 Rapture sold only thirty thousand copies, in contrast to his first book, which reportedly sold more than two million.[3] Apparently readers were thinking, fool me once, shame on you; fool me twice . . .

People continually try to predict when the end will come, but Jesus plainly said, "No one knows." It is like a man who puts servants in charge of his house and then goes away, Jesus said. The man is coming back, but the servants don't know when. The only thing they know for sure is that he will return.[4]

2. Bible prophecy is not as easily interpreted as Bible history.
Biblical prophecy is the inspired prediction of God's determined will in future events. In other words, it is history future. The biblical record of history past has plenty of corroborating evidence in the archives of archaeology and extrabiblical history. For example, we know who the Romans were and what Jerusalem was like in the ancient world. We can go to places the Bible talks about and see a depiction of their cultures and customs, and even most of the events that took place among them, reflected in

---

3   *Ibid., 125.*
4   *Matthew 24:43-51.*

BEFORE AHNULD THE TERMINATOR
MADE FAMOUS THE WORDS
"I'LL BE BACK!," JESUS MADE A
PROMISE TO HIS FOLLOWERS
THAT HE WOULD RETURN
TO EARTH SOMEDAY.

the artifacts we find. But we know virtually nothing of the future world and its cultures. We cannot see them yet. We can only read the descriptions provided for us in Scripture.

The imagery used in the Bible's story of history future complicates matters further. When the biblical prophets had to look into the future to see things they'd never seen before, they did not have the terminology of the familiar. For example, when airplanes flew over one of the few "lost tribes" in the Amazon rainforest, the fliers snapped photographs of a culture that previously had no exposure to the outside civilized world. The pictures are of natives aiming their bows and arrows at the airplanes. If you asked any of these tribesmen what he was firing at, he would not say, "An airplane." He would have no concept of a motorized flying machine piloted by fellow human beings. In his frame of reference, it would be a giant bird or perhaps one of the gods. Or a ghost. He would use the concepts at his disposal to describe something he is clueless about.

Similarly, in the Bible, the prophet Daniel and the apostle John saw visions of things beyond their experience, yet they had to describe them in concepts familiar to them. How would a first-century Jew describe twenty-first-century American cars or computers? The disconnect in familiarity is understandable, but it often complicates interpretation. Nevertheless, while the biblical visions we have are not entirely clear, they are still vivid and colorful. What I'm saying is, basically, it's okay to scratch your head from time to time as you study this stuff.

3. The purpose of knowing the end times is to prepare us. Why did God reveal future world events to us? Was it so that we could have theological arguments about his return? I don't think so. God wants us to trust in his sovereign control of the universe and to look forward to the day of reward that awaits his followers. He has everything well in hand, and he gives us a glimpse of the future to whet our appetites for heaven. While many Christians will come to differing opinions on the finer points of biblical prophecy, and have differences about time frames and even definitions and interpretations, we nearly all agree that the purpose of studying it is not so we'll have a Christian hobby but so we'll get closer to God and get prepared for what he has in store for the future of humankind and the world.[5]

Why Future Events? //

Let's look at some of the reasons why the Bible reveals future events:

1. To keep us from ignorance. First Thessalonians 4:13 says, "Dear brothers and sisters, we want you to know what will happen to the believers who have died so you will not grieve like people who have no hope." God doesn't want you to be uninformed or naive about the future. As a follower of Christ, you should look forward to the reward that awaits you.

2. To motivate us to holy living. Peter wrote, "Since everything around us is going to be destroyed like this, what holy and godly lives you should live, looking forward to the day of God and hurrying it along."[6] When you recognize that this world will be discarded, it puts everything in a different perspective. What really matters is not the temporal possessions or attainments of this world. The real valuables are eternal. How you live is much more important than what you have. This is why Jesus commanded us to lay up our treasures not on earth but in heaven.[7]

3. To encourage us. Paul underscored the comfort of knowing the future. He outlined the events of the future resurrection and then concluded, "So encourage each other with these words."[8] The purpose of biblical revelation is not to help us argue.

---

5   *And as far as hobbies go, end-times speculation is pretty lame.*

6   *2 Peter 3:11-12.*

7   *Matthew 6:19-20.*

8   *1 Thessalonians 4:18.*

Instead, we should thrill at the adventure of the future. Seeing what is to come should encourage us, comfort us, and strengthen us. It should motivate us to commit our lives to God like never before.

The future gives us hope. When our family plans a vacation, I can hardly wait. I look forward to a shift in weather and making memories and eating great food. Every year, once we have the date of our getaway on the calendar, I suddenly have a fresh outlook on life. I work harder. I smile at people. I have something to look forward to.

> THE TIME WE STILL HAVE BEFORE CHRIST'S RETURN ALLOWS MORE OPPORTUNITY FOR THOSE WHO ARE FAR FROM CHRIST TO COME INTO THE KINGDOM. //

Christ followers are headed toward an eternal paradise with God, and just knowing this information should make a huge impact on how we feel about life. As Peter said, "We are looking forward to the new heavens and new earth he has promised, a world filled with God's righteousness."[9]

4. To give us incentive to fulfill our mission. Jesus explained that, before his return, the gospel has to be spread. He said, "The Good News must first be preached to all nations."[10] Knowing the end is imminent brings a sense of urgency to our mission to connect the unconnected to Christ. Think about this: Why did Jesus leave us here? Why did he not take all of his followers directly to heaven? The answer should be obvious—to allow us more time to reach more people. God's heart on the matter is clear: "The Lord isn't really being slow about his promise, as some people think. No, he is being patient for your sake. He does not want anyone

---

9   *2 Peter 3:13.*
10   *Mark 13:10.*

to be destroyed, but wants everyone to repent."[11] The time we still have before Christ's return allows more opportunity for those who are far from Christ to come into the kingdom.

Signs of the Times //
Now that we know why God revealed the future, let's look at the future we need to watch for. If you know how to read the changing signs in the weather, Jesus once remarked, then you should also be able to read the signs of his return.[12] Here is a short list of a few of the signs that precede Jesus' return:

1. Moral decay. Paul painted a pretty dim picture of the last days when writing to Timothy:

> *You should know this, Timothy, that in the last days there will be very difficult times. For people will love only themselves and their money. They will be boastful and proud, scoffing at God, disobedient to their parents, and ungrateful. They will consider nothing sacred. They will be unloving and unforgiving; they will slander others and have no self-control. They will be cruel and hate what is good. They will betray their friends, be reckless, be puffed up with pride, and love pleasure rather than God.*[13]

Cats and dogs living together! Mass hysteria! Doesn't sound too pleasant, does it? Every generation has people who are selfish and criminal, but the last days will be characterized by a society that embraces these sins like never before.

2. Political upheavals and natural disasters. Jesus predicted, "Nation will go to war against nation, and kingdom against

---

11 *2 Peter 3:9.*

12 *Matthew 16:2-3.*

13 *2 Timothy 3:1-4.*

kingdom. There will be famines and earthquakes in many parts of the world. But all this is only the first of the birth pains, with more to come."[14] Certainly the rise in global terrorism and natural tragedies like the 2004 Indian Ocean tsunami or America's Hurricane Katrina demonstrate that the birth pangs are here. As these events escalate, they are like labor pains for the second coming of Christ.

3. Persecution of the followers of Jesus. Jesus forecast in Matthew 24:9, "You will be arrested, persecuted, and killed. You will be hated all over the world because you are my followers." Church history tells us that every generation since the beginning of the church has suffered and many have died for their faith. According to church tradition, most of the twelve disciples died for their faith. In the 20th century alone, it is estimated that around 20 million people died for following Christ. Persecution has been going on since the early church and will not only continue but intensify before he returns.

4. People falling away. Paul told us, "Before that day comes, a couple of things have to happen. First, the Apostasy."[15] The word apostasy means "to forsake" or "to fall away." It is a word often used for divorce. In other words, there will be a decrease of followers of Christ as the end approaches, with many who tagged along with the church for a while essentially filing for divorce from Jesus. As a pastor, I have a hard time imagining that scenario, since I am seeing people come to Christ and grow in their faith every day. But apparently many will fall away. One person in particular will draw worship to himself.

5. The rise of the Anti-Christ. Everyone looks for a savior or a messiah. You don't have to be Jewish to want a hero to step

---

14 *Matthew 24:7-8.*

15 *2 Thessalonians 2:3,* MSG.

forward and make the world a better place. If only someone could deliver the world from poverty and hunger. If only someone could bring world peace and restore us to a prosperous global economy. Sounds like a job for superman . . . or a messiah. And Satan is preparing someone to play that role.

Among the players in the end times is the villain known as the Anti-Christ. Paul warned us about this evil dictator's appearance on the scene of world events in 2 Thessalonians 2:3-4: "Don't be fooled by what they say. For that day will not come until there is a great rebellion against God and the man of lawlessness is revealed—the one who brings destruction. He will exalt himself and defy everything that people call god and every object of worship. He will even sit in the temple of God, claiming that he himself is God." Paul continued to describe this future führer: "This man will come to do the work of Satan with counterfeit power and signs and miracles."[16]

Throughout church history, many have tried to identify the Anti-Christ by reading the signs of the times, a lot like some have tried to predict the timing of Jesus' return. Early Christians might have been inclined to see the Roman emperor Nero or any of his bloodthirsty successors as the Anti-Christ. Others have nominated other world leaders, such as Mussolini, Stalin, and Hitler. In more recent years we've even had some try to identify the Anti-Christ as Ronald Reagan, Mikhail Gorbachev, Saddam Hussein, George W. Bush, and Barack Obama. Even less power-ful leaders like Ted Turner and Bill Gates have been scrutinized for their anti-Christlikeness.

What we learn from the Bible are big-picture thoughts and a few details, but certainly not a name. We should be reluctant to identify the Anti-Christ, especially since it means slandering someone!

Revelation 13 tells us that the Anti-Christ (or "beast") will appear to have some sort of supernatural healing power, that he will astonish the world, that he will have great authority as

---

16 2 Thessalonians 2:9.

THE LORD HIMSELF
WILL COME DOWN
FROM HEAVEN WITH A
COMMANDING SHOUT,
WITH THE VOICE OF THE
ARCHANGEL, AND WITH THE
TRUMPET CALL OF GOD.
1 THESSALONIANS 4:16

a leader in the world and eventually over all the nations of the world, that he will utter blasphemies against God, and that he will literally be worshiped by those who are not followers of Jesus.

As I have mentioned, when John saw visions of this future history, he used the best concepts and terminology at his disposal to describe what he was seeing. So when he said, for instance, that the Anti-Christ comes out of the sea, he may mean that literally the evil one comes up out of an ocean, or he may mean that this man will come to power in a seafaring nation or coastal region, or he may mean symbolically that he arises in an era of utter chaos (since the sea was an important Hebrew symbol representing chaos and trouble).[17] Because we have only John's descriptions (vivid though they are) to go on, Christians have come to many different perspectives on the Anti-Christ. Some say he has already come (Nero or another such leader in the past); some say he will lead a one-world government at some point in the future; and some say he is not a "he" at all but rather a symbol of the general spirit of evil in the world, either throughout all time or as the personification of a greater period of trouble orchestrated by Satan in the end times. It appears evident, however, from how Paul set up the concept of "the man of lawlessness" before John's vision, that what we are reading about is a real person—one in a time future to Paul. (Which means Nero is likely out, but Bill Gates is still in contention. Just kidding.)

FOR THOSE WHO
CRY OUT FOR JUSTICE,
THE LORD WILL
BRING IT, AND HE WILL
BRING IT MIGHTILY. //

---

17 *Revelation 13:1.*

The Rapture //

The Rapture is the moment in the end times when Jesus will return in the sky to gather up those who believe in him and rescue them from the great time of trouble on the earth. Because of the divergent details the Bible gives us on this event, Christians have developed different perspectives that can be boiled down to three major views.

In the *posttribulational Rapture* view, the Rapture is seen as taking place after the seven-year tribulation foretold in the book of Daniel and by Jesus (in Matthew 24, for example) and depicted in the book of Revelation. Posttribulationists believe that Jesus will return at the end of the time of trouble to Rapture the church and that the Rapture is either simultaneous with the "official" second coming of Christ or else separated from it by only a small matter of time.

Adherents to the *midtribulational Rapture* view believe that the Rapture will occur at some point during the seven-year tribulation. Not all believe (as the name of the view suggests) that it will be at the exact midpoint, but rather at some time during the great distress. Within this view is a related view—something of a merging of midtribulationism and posttribulationism—called the "pre-wrath Rapture" view, which has enjoyed some popularity in the last decade or so.

The inherent problem with these two views is that both place the Rapture after some discernible events that would nullify the "suddenness" the Bible tells us characterizes the Rapture. We can't believe the Rapture can happen at any moment if we suddenly have an observable time line in the tribulation.

The third view, and by far the most dominant view of the evangelical church, is called the *pretribulational Rapture* view. This is the view depicted, for instance, in the popular book series *Left Behind* by Tim LaHaye and Jerry Jenkins. In the pretribulational perspective, the Rapture occurs at a sudden moment that precedes and precipitates the great tribulation.

Paul described the Rapture this way: "The Lord himself will come down from heaven with a commanding shout, with the voice of the archangel, and with the trumpet call of God. First, the Christians who have died will rise from their graves. Then, together with them, we who are still alive and remain on the earth will be caught up in the clouds to meet the Lord in the air. Then we will be with the Lord forever."[18]

As I've said, the Rapture is the belief that the Lord will come in the clouds and snatch the church away. Those Christians who are dead will be resurrected from the grave and reunited with their spirit. Those who have not died will be instantly changed and never experience death. That sounds pretty sweet to me!

The Rapture is not the same as the second coming, however. After the church is raptured, and after a period of tribulation on the earth (during which some may choose to forsake the beast and accept Christ), Jesus will return again, this time finally and victoriously to establish his literal, permanent, eternal reign over all. This is the view that I've come to hold as I study what the Bible teaches.

There are many opinions and interpretations about the Rapture and I respect my friends and mentors who hold divergent views. Many throughout history have held to an amillenial perspective of Revelation. This view sees the Rapture and the second coming of Jesus as the same thing. It takes a more symbolic interpretation of Revelation believed to be more appropriate to the apocalyptic genre of literature that Revelation represents. Augustine and many leaders of the Reformation held to this perspective.

There is much more that could be said, and many other interpretations. What everyone agrees on is that while the first coming of Christ was hardly noticed when a baby was born to a humble couple and laid in a lowly manger, the next time he comes the whole world will take notice!

---

18 *1 Thessalonians 4:16-17.*

Warrior Jesus //

We get our view of Jesus from the Gospels, which are powerful and compassionate in their view of Jesus on earth. But we also have another picture in the Bible—that of Revelation, where we see Jesus coming in glory and power. This is how all history ends, with the climactic crash of Jesus into earth, kicking butt and taking names.

The book of Revelation is full of symbols, many of which are confusing and cryptic. But the book does not hide for one verse, one sentence, one word that it is about the grand appearing of the undeniable Lord of the universe. Revelation 1:1 informs us right off the bat that the book is "a revelation from Jesus Christ." It is about Jesus and his exaltation. We don't know the day or the hour of his return, but we do know that when he returns it will not be as a humble peasant but as an exalted warrior. When you look to Revelation 19, it describes him arriving on a white horse, bold and brazen:

> *I saw heaven opened, and a white horse was standing there. Its rider was named Faithful and True, for he judges fairly and wages a righteous war.... The armies of heaven, dressed in the finest of pure white linen, followed him on white horses. . . . He will release the fierce wrath of God, the Almighty, like juice flowing from a winepress. On his robe at his thigh was written this title: King of all kings and Lord of all lords.[19]*

What an entrance! For those who cry out for justice, the Lord will bring it, and he will bring it mightily. Mark Driscoll and Gerry Breshears elaborate:

> Jesus is not revealed as a glass-jawed hippie wearing a dress. Rather, he is an Ultimate Fighter warrior king with a

---

19 *Revelation 19:11, 14-16.*

tattoo down his leg who rides into battle against Satan, sin, and death on a trusty horse, just like every decent Western from Pecos Bill to the Rifleman, the Cisco Kid, the Lone Ranger, Buffalo Bill, and Wild Bill Hickok. If we were to see Jesus today, we would see him in glory, not in humility. We would see a Jesus who will never take a beating again, but is coming to open a can on the unrepentant until their blood flows upon the earth like grapes crushed in the violence of a winepress.[20]

This can be a overwhelming thought, but Jesus is filled with both love and justice, and the Bible teaches that he will return to judge the earth.

Here Comes the Judge //

Over the years, I have worked my share of summer church camps. At one camp I was amazed at how well the kids were responding to my authority. When I told them to do something, they did it. When I told them it was time for bed, they went to bed. When I told them to take showers and clean up, they took showers.

Just as I was starting to get used to this radical behavior, one of the kids came up to me and said, "Sir, since you are the judge, what happens if we get in trouble?"

"What do you mean?" I asked.

"Well, everybody calls you 'Judge,' " he said. "I was wondering what you do to us if we mess up."

Suddenly it all clicked for me. The kids had heard my name as Judge instead of Jud. That was why they were jumping at my every word!

But Jesus will not suffer from mistaken identity. He is the judge, and he *will* judge. Listen carefully to what happens on judgment day:

---

20 *Mark Driscoll and Gerry Breshears,* Vintage Jesus: Timeless Answers to Timely Questions *(Wheaton, IL: Good News, 2008), 150.*

I saw a great white throne and the one sitting on it. The earth and sky fled from his presence, but they found no place to hide. I saw the dead, both great and small, standing before God's throne. And the books were opened, including the Book of Life. And the dead were judged according to what they had done, as recorded in the books. . . . And anyone whose name was not found recorded in the Book of Life was thrown into the lake of fire.[21]

While this may seem terrifying, it is intended to be good news for believers. Their names are in the Book of Life. They have received forgiveness and grace. On the last day, the wrongs will be made right. All the misuse of justice, all the horrible things done by people to others, will be dealt with either through Jesus and his sacrifice or through one's personal accountability. No matter how bad it gets here on earth, we look forward to that day when God will set the record straight. Paul said, "What we suffer now is nothing compared to the glory he will reveal to us later."[22]

Hang in there, friend. The future is worth waiting for.

GOD'S TIMETABLE
AND MY TIMETABLE
ARE DIFFERENT.
BUT I KNOW THIS: HE WILL
SHOW UP EXACTLY ON TIME. //

Not an Inconvenience //

When I was fifteen, I heard someone talk on Christ's return being imminent. I remember thinking, *No, that can't be. I have to get my driver's license first.* I was thinking of Jesus coming back like it was some huge inconvenience in my life. As if the restoration of all things and being with him face to face somehow paled in

---

21 *Revelation 20:11-12, 15.*

22 *Romans 8:18.*

comparison with being able to drive a car. Have you ever been there?

After I got my driver's license, I was pulled over one day. I thought I was in trouble for a lot more than a speeding ticket, and as the police officer walked up to my car, I prayed, "Okay, Jesus, you can come now! Please! Please come now! Anytime in the next ten seconds would be great!"

God's timetable and my timetable are different. But I know this: he will show up exactly on time.

Until that day, let's use the Bible's information to encourage each other, to look forward with anticipation to our heavenly home, and to live for eternal reasons. Between that time and this present time, we must share the message of what Jesus has done.

Discussion Questions

1. *What do you dwell on most: Jesus' first coming or his second coming? Why?*

2. *Do you find hope in the knowledge of Jesus' return? How does a study of end times affect you?*

3. *Read Acts 1:7 and Matthew 24:42. Why is it pointless to argue about the specific dates and times of coming events?*

4. *Compare 1 Corinthians 15:51-52 with 1 Thessalonians 4:13-17. What is Paul revealing about the future?*

5. *What does it mean to live with anticipation of Jesus' return in your life this week?*

KNOCKIN' ON HEAVEN'S (OR HELL'S) DOOR //

✳ ✳ ✳ Before I became a Christian, whenever I'd hear Christians talk about heaven and hell, I didn't think hell sounded so bad. If hell was real, and the Christians were right, then all my friends would end up there anyway. Hell sounded like one big party. And if heaven was populated by some of the people who claimed they knew how to get there, I wasn't sure I wanted to be with them. They sounded judgmental and kinda boring.

I could never quite wrap my mind around their idea of God. Something didn't jibe. Christians claimed God was loving, but they also claimed he would torture me forever in endless pain in hell if I didn't believe in him. That didn't sound too loving. He sounded like the Grinch, only meaner and less cool.

By that very incomprehensible grace of God, I eventually became a Christian, but my wrestling with the Bible's teaching on heaven and hell did not end.

Statistically speaking, the majority of Americans actually believe in the existence of heaven and hell. According to a poll by the Barna Group, 76 percent of people believe in heaven and 64 percent believe they will go there. Meanwhile, 71 percent of people believe in a hell, but—surprise, surprise—only one half of 1 percent think they'll go there.[1] A lot of people think that they're bad and that there's a bad place where bad people go after death, but hardly anyone thinks they personally qualify.

Anecdotally, we hear a lot about the afterlife in the form of so-called near-death experiences. Many people who have been clinically dead and then resuscitated report having seen a bright

---

1   Barna Group, "Americans Describe Their Views About Life and Death," October 21, 2003, http://www.barna.org/barna-update/article/5-barna-update/128-americans-describe-their-views-about-life-after-death.

light or felt a sense of euphoric calm. Rarely do these reports of afterlife snapshots include glimpses of hell, but occasionally they do. Cardiologist Maurice Rawlings has given the account of a patient who, in the middle of an attempt to resuscitate him by heart massage, began to cry out in terror, "Don't stop! . . . Each time you quit, I go back to hell! Don't let me go back to hell!"[2]

Rawlings reports that some people who go through such terrifying near-death experiences are so impacted that they eventually become Christians.[3] I guess they've literally had the hell scared out of them.

What's Down with Hell? //

Our culture has gotten a lot of mileage out of hellish terminology. Colleges have hell week as people are pledging to different fraternities. There's also hell week in football and other industries and enterprises when things get really intense for a particular week. There's the Hell's Angels motorcycle gang as well as the related phrase "hell on wheels," and in New York there is even an area of town called Hell's Kitchen.

People also apply hell personally when they say, "My job is hell" or "My marriage is hell." And I've even heard someone say that something "smelled like hell." I'm not sure what hell smells like, but I get the impression it's not good. (Maybe if the rumors of sulfur in hell are true, it smells like rotten eggs?)

I recently visited the largest landfill in America, just outside of Las Vegas, because one of the terms Jesus used for hell recalls a garbage dump. When Jesus referenced hell, he used a couple of different words. One word is *Hades*, employed in the story of Lazarus in Luke 16. Hades was used to refer to the place where people go prior to final judgment in hell. But the other term he used that we translate as "hell" in English is the

---

2   Quoted in Tillman Rodabough and Kyle Cole, "Near-Death Experiences as Secular Eschatology," in The Handbook of Death and Dying, ed. Clifton D. Bryant (Thousand Oaks, CA: Sage, 2003), 1:140.

3   Maurice Rawlings, To Hell and Back: Life After Death—Startling New Evidence (Nashville: Thomas Nelson, 1996).

Greek word *Gehenna*, which has its origins in reference to the city dump. *Gehenna* refers to a narrow ravine south of Jerusalem. Fires continually smoldered there, as the site was used as a burning ground for waste and trash. In time, the valley became so noxious that its name became a synonym for hell. At one time, Jewish tradition even held that the entrance to hell began in that valley.

There are lots of things in a landfill, from scrap metal to old kitchen appliances, from dinner tables to diapers, things that should be recycled and things recycling centers wouldn't touch with a ten-foot pole. Rats fester in landfills, and there can be as many maggots as there are grains of sand on a beach. A couple of things happen in such a place: disintegration and isolation. And these are the two metaphors the Bible uses to describe the eternal garbage dump that is hell—fire and darkness. Fire disintegrates and darkness isolates.[4] The short definition of hell is a place of utter separation from the love of God—the "outer darkness," as Jesus called it.[5]

Hell Is Hell //

While we may not be able to get as clear a picture of hell from the Bible as if we were documentary makers with video cameras, the imagery we do get is enough to piece together a rather terrifying landscape. Any one of the images is frightening by itself. Put together, the composite is . . . well, *hellish*.

Some may argue that hell is only a metaphor or a symbol, that it is not a real place with real torment. But even if the descriptions we get in the Bible are symbolic in themselves, it does not necessarily follow that the place called hell is symbolic. In fact, it doesn't make much sense to have all kinds of warnings against a place that is going to be painful and dark if such a place doesn't exist. Do pain and fire make sense as symbols of eternal sleep or some other unpainful, unfiery eternities? No.

---

4   *Tim Keller,* The Reason for God: Belief in an Age of Skepticism *(New York: Dutton, 2008), 259.*

5   *Matthew 8:12; 22:13; 25:30.*

Regardless of whether hell is a place with literal fire in it, or whether it's even a literal *location* or not, it is nevertheless clearly a place where unredeemed people go and where the experience feels beyond terrible.

IF HELL WERE NOT A LITERAL
PLACE OF CONSCIOUS TORMENT,
IT MAKES LITTLE SENSE FOR
JESUS TO HAVE TALKED ABOUT IT
AS IF IT WERE. //

The Bible tells us hell will be a place of fire, destruction, torment, and punishment.[6] This is not an environment where any parties are going to be taking place, contrary to my youthful speculation (and the lyrical musings of AC/DC). There will be an interminable darkness in hell, and the pain and despair is such that it leads to "weeping and gnashing of teeth."[7]

The glimpses we get of what hell will be like are enough to tell us that we should neither want to go there nor be ambivalent about others going there. We do not know exactly what it feels like to be hit by a speeding train, but we know enough from the available evidence that we do not want to be caught on the tracks when one is coming. And should we encounter someone who is caught on the tracks in that situation, it is okay to knock that person out of the way.

If hell were not a literal place of conscious torment, it makes little sense for Jesus to have talked about it as if it were. We can always count on Jesus to tell us truthful things, to not lead our theology astray. And even when things he says are difficult to grasp intellectually, it is not because he wants us to believe the opposite of what he's saying or implying. If hell were not a place you wouldn't want to go, he would not talk about it in the terms he does.

---

6 Fire: Matthew 5:22; 18:9; Mark 9:43. Destruction: Matthew 10:28. Torment: Luke 16:23. Punishment: Matthew 23:33; 2 Peter 2:4.

7 Matthew 8:12.

Therein lies another logical point for belief in hell as a literal place of real torment: we do not believe heaven is a metaphor. Whatever heaven is like, we trust that it is a real "place" where we will be really present with Jesus, seeing him face to face and enjoying the company of the triune God and the eternal fellowship of believers. If heaven is real, it makes sense that hell is real as well. And that is what makes hell truly hellish—not just the pain and the darkness but the fact that in hell we will experience eternal disfellowship with God.

Hell and the Undoing of Ourselves //

When the Bible talks about hell, it never says it was created for people, but rather that it was created for Satan and his demons. But hell is apparently a reality people will face, as Jesus warns us in several passages of the Bible.

The question most of us end up pondering at some point in our lives, though, is how a loving God could send people to such a place of disintegration and isolation.

The Bible says God "does not want anyone to be destroyed, but wants everyone to repent" and he "sent his Son into the world not to judge the world, but to save the world through him."[8] If this is true, how does anyone end up in hell? Perhaps God doesn't so much send people to hell as people send themselves there. Hell is the default destination of the sinful heart, and since we are all born with original sin, every person without exception deserves hell. Because God is holy and just, he would be well within his rights to send us all to hell in one very large hand basket. But because God is love, he sent his Son to secure redemption for all who would repent of their sin and trust him for salvation. That's the way out of hell. The way in is simply to do nothing at all, to maintain earthly business as usual, trusting anything and everything but God.

C. S. Lewis writes, "There are only two kinds of people in the end: those who say to God, 'Thy will be done,' and those to whom God says, in the end, 'Thy will be done.' All that are in hell,

---

8 *2 Peter 3:9; John 3:17.*

choose it. Without that self-choice there could be no Hell."[9]

When we live our lives with ourselves at the center, with our own values and preferences and desires as our greatest goods, and with our own efforts as our means to our own version of heaven, we get the result of our efforts to live apart from God and his ways: an eternity apart from God. It's a fair trade, but not one any of us should want.

One thing that struck me on my visit to the dump, besides the smell, was that most of the things that were there were not created to be there. They were made for a purpose, and rotting away in a landfill wasn't it. In a similar way God created humanity for the purpose of knowing and loving him, of being in a relationship with him. Jesus went through hell so that we could exchange hell for heaven.

Some have suggested that hell is simply our chosen identity taken into eternity. When we engage in self-absorption and turn from God in our lives, we experience damage from that. It's like finally getting the reward we've put on layaway and have been paying installments on all along.

It was Johnny Cash who said all of his years wrestling with an addiction to pills were an effort to get back to the high he felt from the first pill. And every pill he took ultimately separated him from himself, from his family, and from God. There was the disintegration of his life from his addiction and there was also isolation. Now imagine that personal disintegration and isolation going on forever. Eventually all traces of being made in the image of God would be obscured by one's own self-made and self-actualized humanity.

Those who end up in hell do so because they have, in willful opposition to Jesus' admonition to lay up treasures in heaven, expressly done the opposite and laid up their treasures in hell.[10] As N. T. Wright says, "With the death of that body in which they inhabited God's good world, in which the flickering flame of goodness

---

9 C. S. Lewis, The Great Divorce *(New York: HarperCollins, 2001), 75.*
10 *Matthew 6:20.*

had not been completely snuffed out, they pass simultaneously not only beyond hope but also beyond pity."[11] The hellbound go further into delusion, selfishness, and self-absorption.

C. S. Lewis captures this idea in his imaginative elaboration on the afterlife, *The Great Divorce*:

> The whole difficulty of understanding Hell is that the thing to be understood is so nearly Nothing. But ye'll have had experiences . . . it begins with a grumbling mood, and yourself still distinct from it: perhaps critising it. And yourself, in a dark hour, may will that mood, embrace it. Ye can repent and come out of it again. But there may come a day when you can do that no longer. Then there will be no *you* left to criticise the mood, nor even to enjoy it, but just the grumble itself going on forever like a machine.[12]

Elsewhere Lewis writes, "It is not a question of God 'sending' us to Hell. In each of us there is something growing up which will of itself *be* hell unless it is nipped in the bud."[13]

Judging Judgment //

In the Bible, hell is a reality. We like to think that a God of judgment could never be a God of love. Yet all loving people are sometimes filled with anger and wrath, sometimes precisely *because* of their love. Anger is not the opposite of love; hate is. God gets angry because he loves passionately. He hates injustice because he loves justice. He hates abuse because he loves peace. He hates divorce because he loves reconciliation. He hates evil because he loves good. He hates sin because he loves holiness. He hates Cheez Whiz because he loves actual food.

This sort of dichotomy is not a foreign concept to us, even

---

11 N. T. Wright, Surprised by Hope: Rethinking Heaven, the Resurrection, and the Mission of the Church *(New York: HarperOne, 2008), 182.*

12 C. S. Lewis, The Great Divorce *(New York: HarperCollins, 2001), 77–78.*

13 C. S. Lewis, "The Trouble with 'X,' " in God in the Dock: Essays on Theology and Ethics *(Grand Rapids, MI: Eerdmans, 1994), 155.*

to the atheists among us. We get our innate sense of justice from being made in the image of a just and righteous God. But you don't have to believe in God to hate murder, because you love life. Or to be angry about someone harming your children, because you love your family. When you get down to it, nearly everyone affirms justice in some sense. If there were never any judgment of anyone for anything, our world would be pretty screwed up.

Yale theologian Miroslav Volf is a Croatian immigrant who survived the violence of the Balkans. Volf suggests that the idea that God doesn't judge only makes sense in the safety of the Western suburbs.[14] In an area stricken with violence, the only way violence ends is when a person comes to believe that God will work it out and they don't have to. Volf goes on to conclude that the idea that God would never judge (because he is love) will actually foster more violence in the world.

Randy Alcorn notes, "The best of life on Earth is a glimpse of Heaven; the worst of life is a glimpse of Hell."[15] For some, this earth will be the closest they ever come to hell; for others, it will be as close as they ever come to heaven.

And the difference, like the proverbial fork in the road, is the cross of Jesus Christ. In essence, many of us say to the idea of thinking and living on God's terms, "Over my dead body . . ." Yet Jesus died on the cross and said in effect, "No, over my dead body." He lay himself down as a barrier to hell. We can either accept his death as our substitute and atonement or we can step over his body to continue on our self-centered and self-interested journey. As the Bible predicts, the message of the cross is foolishness to some people.[16]

The Christian idea of justification by faith can infuriate. We posted a video on YouTube that showed people being accepted into heaven based on their faith rather than their works.[17] The

---

14 *Miroslav Volf,* Exclusion and Embrace: A Theological Exploration of Identity, Otherness, and Reconciliation *(Nashville: Abingdon, 1996), 303–4.*

15 *Randy Alcorn,* Heaven *(Carol Stream, IL: Tyndale, 2004), 28.*

16 *1 Corinthians 1:18.*

17 *"The Good-O-Meter," YouTube, May 12, 2007, http://www.youtube.com/watch?v=XrLzYw6ULYw.*

comments on the video are quite revealing. One person wrote, "This is sick and perverted. No matter how many people you kill, how many children you rape, how much you steal, how evil a person you are, you'll get your salvation if you happen to believe in the right God. And Gandhi, you evil heretic, burn in hell!"

Another person commented, "Just who's point is this proving? It is utterly amazing to me that any Christian could think this is a good thing. Where is there morality when any sin can be forgiven? Who wants to go to a heaven populated by criminals and reprobates?"

In a self-obsessed world, we acknowledge that there is badness in the world—we just don't think we're responsible for it. Other people are bad, not us. Or we don't have to be good necessarily, just better than whoever is really bad. In this spiritual economy, Adolf Hitler and Jeffrey Dahmer go to hell, because their sin is measurably bad and deserving of it. The rest of us are on a sliding scale.

But that is not the way the Bible says sin works. Sin is inside us. It is a condition of the heart that deserves judgment, no matter how well we're able to manage it.

And it's not the way salvation works either. We cannot do enough good works to overcome the sin in us. How do we know when enough is enough? Do we just ballpark it? No, the sin in us deserves the wrath of God that only perfect obedience can appease. Either way you look at that, it is bad news. But the Bible is not a bad-news book. The good news is that Jesus obeyed perfectly on our behalf and absorbed the wrath of God on our behalf. If we will trust his works and his sacrifice, we will be justified by our just God. It may sound crazy, but trying to achieve heaven any other way is true insanity.

THE CONDITION OF HEAVEN IS RESTORATION—
PEACE WHERE THERE WAS TURMOIL,
COMFORT WHERE THERE WAS PAIN,
PURITY WHERE THERE WAS SIN,
AND JOY WHERE THERE WAS GRIEF. //

Highway to Heaven //

The highway to hell is not a highway we want to be on, so what about the stairway to heaven? What does the Bible say about heaven? The book of Revelation describes it this way: "God's home is now among his people! He will live with them, and they will be his people. God himself will be with them. He will wipe every tear from their eyes, and there will be no more death or sorrow or crying or pain. All these things are gone forever."[18]

The condition of heaven is restoration—peace where there was turmoil, comfort where there was pain, purity where there was sin, and joy where there was grief. This is everlasting life. But the greatest gift of heaven is the presence of God. The ultimate promise is this: "God himself will be with them." We will never get over the nearness of God. That feeling of comfort and assurance will never leave us for all eternity.

When it comes to heaven, the Bible says, "No eye has seen, no ear has heard, and no mind has imagined what God has prepared for those who love him."[19] You ain't seen nothing yet. I always took this to mean that we couldn't know much of anything about heaven. We were just left with a mystery this side of Jesus' second coming. But I never really noticed the very next verse: "But it was to us that God revealed these things by his Spirit."[20]

This passage is not actually saying that we can't know anything about heaven; it is saying the opposite. We can know some things about heaven because God has revealed them. As you read on, it becomes clear that God has revealed them though his Word.

In fact, the Bible challenges us to meditate on the prospect of heaven: "Since you have been raised to new life with Christ, set your sights on the realities of heaven, where Christ sits in the place of honor at God's right hand."[21] The phrase "set your

---

18 *Revelation 21:3-4.*

19 *1 Corinthians 2:9.*

20 *1 Corinthians 2:10.*

21 *Colossians 3:1.*

sights" literally means to seek, to engage in a diligent and single-minded pursuit. And it is in the present tense, which suggests an active search. We should keep seeking heaven and learning about heaven. We'll spend more than trillions of years exploring heaven in eternity and still not reach the border of its pleasures.

Heaven FAQ's //

Because of the profound promise of heaven, many of us naturally have questions about it right now. I once solicited questions on heaven and the afterlife and received hundreds of responses. Here is a sampling of the head scratchers and some no-spin answers:

1. Am I going to be bored in heaven? What do we do all day—play the harp? If we get our theology from a Tom and Jerry cartoon, we'd have to answer yes to this question. For years I thought we'd just float around on clouds in togas and sing songs all the time. The idea of singing forever in a heavenly diaper of some kind did not cause me to look forward to heaven. (I actually had a choir teacher tell me to lip-sync on a choir tour! My voice wasn't cut out for the glee club, much less the hallowed halls of heaven.)

I once read on a Starbucks cup this quote from Joel Stein, a columnist for the *LA Times*, which captures this sentiment:

> Heaven is totally overrated. It seems boring. Clouds, listening to people play the harp. It should be somewhere you can't wait to go, like a luxury hotel. Maybe blue skies and soft music were enough to keep people in line in the 17th century, but Heaven has to step it up a bit. They're basically getting by because they only have to be better than Hell.

But the reality of heaven is quite different from many of our cultural portraits and understandings. The Bible describes

WE'LL SPEND MORE THAN
TRILLIONS OF YEARS
EXPLORING HEAVEN AND
STILL NOT REACH THE BORDERS
OF ITS PLEASURES.

heaven in breathtaking terms. The Bible talks about a new heaven and a new earth, telling us that the current earth will be destroyed by fire and that a new earth will be created for us to live on. So we won't be floating around in the clouds; we'll have new bodies and we'll live on a new earth that is similar to but different from (and far better than) our current earth. We see in the Bible that there won't be any pain or mourning or loss. We read about a stream and a forest inside of a city, the New Jerusalem, that will be there.

In heaven we will always be learning, growing, and discovering. Paul told us, "God raised us up with Christ and seated us with him in the heavenly realms in Christ Jesus, in order that in the coming ages he might show the incomparable riches of his grace, expressed in his kindness to us in Christ Jesus."[22] The wording of the phrase "in the coming ages" seems to imply this will be a progressive revelation as we learn more and more throughout eternity.

Some research suggests that even now we use only ten percent of our brainpower. Imagine using one hundred percent or more on the new earth. There is nothing in the Bible to suggest that we will peak mentally in heaven. We will have new bodies, so it stands to reason that we can learn and grow and develop for eternity.

And I believe we will work. God created work and said it was good. God himself is a God who works. In Genesis, when humankind sinned, God did not curse work. He cursed the ground that the humans will work. Work itself is a great thing. It has been estimated there are more than fifty thousand occupations in the United States. Yet how many people do you know who are truly satisfied with their jobs? There are personnel problems, lack of adequate pay, long hours, and monotonous tasks. And then just the physical and mental exertion. Over and over again, people find themselves doing things they do not enjoy. But those problems will all be behind us in heaven.

---

22 *Ephesians 2:6-7, NIV.*

Anthony Hoekema writes:

The possibilities that now rise before us boggle the mind. Will there be "better Beethovens" on the new earth?...better Rembrandts, better Raphaels? Shall we read better poetry, better drama, and better prose? Will scientists continue to advance in the technological achievement, will geologists continue to dig out the treasures of the earth, and will architects continue to build imposing and attractive structures? Will there be exciting new adventures in space travel? . . . Our culture will glorify God in ways that surpass our most fantastic dreams.[23]

We will see many of our unrealized dreams on earth fulfilled in heaven. It will be amazing. There will be pleasure there and perhaps some great food! In Revelation 19:9 the Bible promises the wedding supper of the Lamb! The food at the reception should be killer, better than anything we've ever enjoyed.

We will also worship. But worship is more than just singing songs; it is celebrating all that God is with all that we are. Heaven will be a place of discovery, learning, growing, and changing for the better, but without sin and pain. We'll have fun.

2. Do you go to heaven right away after you die, or do you wait until the second coming of Christ? Christians have differing opinions here, and that is okay. But as I read the Bible, it seems that when we die we are immediately in God's presence. After all, Jesus told the thief on the cross, "*Today* you will be with me in paradise."[24] And Paul assumed that to be "away from these earthly bodies" is to "be at home with the Lord."[25]

---

23 Anthony Hoekema, "Heaven: Not Just an Eternal Day Off," Christianity Today, June 6, 2003, http://www. christianitytoday.com/ct/2003/122/54.0.html.

24 Luke 23:43, emphasis added.

25 2 Corinthians 5:8.

But none of this means we are in heaven in its completed form.

The Bible speaks of the future and of a new heaven and new earth where we will live with God forever. Randy Alcorn sets up a helpful distinction between the "intermediate heaven" and "heaven." The "intermediate heaven" is where we go when we die and we are in the presence of God. "Heaven" refers to the new heaven and the new earth as a physical place where we will dwell with God forever. This new heaven and new earth are still to come.

Alcorn gives a great analogy that I'll adjust a little. Say you live in Vegas and you are thrilled to find out that you inherited an awesome beach house in Miami. The house comes with a job you will love, and your best friend just happens to live right down the street. You send all your stuff ahead and go to the airport to fly to your new life and your new house. Unfortunately your flight has a stop in Denver, Colorado, on the way to Miami. There you will meet up with some friends and travel on together to Miami. When you walk up to the ticket counter in Vegas and the agent asks you where you are headed, you don't say Denver. That is a stop along the way. You say you are headed to Miami. Well, the intermediate heaven is like the layover in Denver (without the airport's jacked-up prices[26]), and heaven is like the ultimate destination in Miami.

During this "layover," we are in God's presence. We are spiritual beings. Our physical body remains in the grave and our spirit returns to the God who gave it. Our spirits will remain with God, separated from our physical bodies, until the resurrection on the day when the Lord returns.

Now, there are also different opinions on whether we will be only spiritual in form or whether we may have some tangible form. Nobody knows for sure. But what is clear in the Bible is that when Christ returns we will be given a new, resurrected body: "Our earthly bodies are planted in the ground when we

---

26 *Seriously, eight dollars for bottled water?*

die, but they will be raised to live forever. Our bodies are buried in brokenness, but they will be raised in glory. They are buried in weakness, but they will be raised in strength."[27]

When Christ returns, our bodies will be raised and will be joined with our spirits and we will receive a new body. Until then, the Bible seems to teach, we will be alive with Christ.

3. Will I be able to see things or people on earth from heaven?
When we pull together the pertinent teachings in the Bible, the answer to this question appears to be yes. Consider Jesus' words, "There is more joy in heaven over one lost sinner who repents and returns to God than over ninety-nine others who are righteous and haven't strayed away." Notice he did not say that just the angels rejoice, but that there is joy in heaven. Later he said there is "joy in the presence of God's angels."[28] Who is rejoicing in the presence of God's angels? I take this to mean that people who are with God are rejoicing when someone turns to God. They are rejoicing when family members and friends turn to him.

While some may disagree, I view the teaching of the Bible to imply that we can see from heaven—the intermediate heaven— what is happening on earth. We'll be aware.

4. Do we live with our family members as a family in heaven?
A new body and a new home would be incomplete without our family and friends. Heaven will be one huge family reunion.

One of the questions we inevitably wrestle with is "Will we recognize our friends in heaven?" Jesus gives us some insight into this. Once, as he was talking with a group of religious leaders, he said, "As to whether there will be a resurrection of the dead—haven't you ever read about this in the Scriptures? Long after Abraham, Isaac, and Jacob had died, God said, 'I am the God of Abraham, the God of Isaac, and the God of Jacob.' So he

---

27 *1 Corinthians 15:42-43.*
28 *Luke 15:7, 10.*

is the God of the living, not the dead."[29] Jesus pointed to the fact that Abraham, Isaac, and Jacob are still living and that they still have their identity.

> THERE WILL BE
> NO MORE GOODBYES,
> NO MORE ABRUPT
> ENDINGS. //

In heaven, it appears, we will keep our identity. Just as we will be able to recognize Abraham, Isaac, and Jacob, so we will be able to recognize the people we know and love. We can look forward to conversations with loved ones as well as people who have died throughout all of human history. Imagine talking with Moses or Abraham or a believer from the Middle Ages!

Over the years, I have done my share of funerals and have witnessed lots of families mourning and grieving. It will be awesome in heaven to also witness these families experiencing the restoration of eternal life. I want to be there when those families are reunited, when their crying is turned to rejoicing, when the relationships that were halted begin again. Wives will be reunited with their husbands. Children will be reunited with their parents. Friends and associates will rejoice in seeing each other again. There will be no more goodbyes, no more abrupt endings.

Maybe some of the people you loved the most in this world have already gone ahead of you, and they're waiting for you. When they died, something within you died and you haven't felt whole since. The feeling you have within you is a homesick feeling, and you've felt that way for a long time. Yet, one day soon—in just a moment from now, according to God's view of time—you will be reunited. Until then, allow that homesick feeling to focus your attention on your heavenly home.

---

29 *Matthew 22:31-32.*

5. Will we know that our unsaved loved ones are not there? Will we feel sad for that? This is a difficult question to answer. I believe we will certainly know that our unsaved loved ones are not in heaven. In heaven we will have greater knowledge, not less, and certainly our happiness in heaven will not be based on ignorance of what is really happening. Yet we also know there won't be crying or pain.[30] Somehow God, who is "the Father of compassion and the God of all comfort, who comforts us in all our troubles," will be able to heal this sorrow.[31] This is hard for us to understand on this side of heaven. It is a promise we have to hold on to by faith.

6. Is there baseball in heaven? Of course! The book of Genesis begins with a description of baseball. Genesis begins with the words "In the big inning."

Bad jokes aside, I believe it is likely that physical sports and activities will exist in heaven. If God designed our bodies to engage in all sorts of physical activities, and he gave us the capacity to enjoy games and sports here on earth, why would he not allow that enjoyment to continue in heaven? Since athletic activity and competition are not inherently sinful, there is no reason to believe that these same kinds or similar activities will not exist in heaven.

If baseball does exist in heaven, where everything is perfect, I think it will be even better than it is here. The Yankees won't be allowed to spend twice as much on their payroll as other teams. Steroids won't be used, because our bodies will already be perfect. Vin Scully and Harry Caray will announce all the games. The fields will be perfect. The umpires will make all the right calls. The days will all be sunny. And the Angels will always make it to the playoffs. Play ball!

---

30 *1 Corinthians 13:12; Revelation 21:4.*

31 *2 Corinthians 1:3-4, NIV.*

REMEMBER THAT GOD
DOES TRULY FORGIVE
AND HEAVEN IS A
PERFECT PLACE.
THE PAIN AND HARDSHIP
OF EARTH WILL ONLY
MAKE HEAVEN MORE
WONDERFUL.

7. Will we see our aborted child in heaven? (I know for me, it has taken me so many years to be able to talk about it, and through these years, I've found many women who just can't even deal with it.) I am sorry for the pain that so many feel in connection with this question. And I know the sense of loss applies both to aborted children and to those lost in childbirth. One of my sisters, Rebecca, passed away hours after she was born. The pain of this loss is something my family carried deeply.

Since God forms us in our mother's womb and knows us before we are even born,[32] babies who have died were still formed and known by God. While some may disagree, I believe based on the character of God these lost little ones can be healed permanently when we get to heaven.

As we've seen, the Bible alludes to the fact that we will be able to know people and recognize them in heaven and that we retain our individual characteristics as a person. So even though we may not have physically met a child here on earth, we could meet and know the child in heaven. I believe it will be a wonderful and joyful reunion.[33]

Guilt and grief will no longer mar such a relationship. Remember that God does truly forgive and heaven is a perfect place. The pain and hardship of earth will only make heaven more wonderful. Perhaps your child will grab your hand and be the first to show you around his or her home in heaven. I believe I'll meet my sister there.

A great deal of the pain that we experience in life is the result of sin. Some of the pain comes from our own sin, some comes from the sin of others, and still other pain comes from the fallen nature of the world we live in, the universal brokenness that resulted from the Fall. Often we experience great sadness as a result of the sinful actions of another person: the betrayal of a spouse, the rebellion of a child, the lie of a friend, the act of a terrorist. Other times, we were the ones who betrayed or rebelled or

---

32 *Psalm 139:13.*

33 *1 Thessalonians 4:14-18.*

lied or committed violence that not only hurt others but also left us with feelings of guilt, shame, and sorrow.

God has a different plan for heaven! The Bible tells us that heaven is a place where "there will be no more death or mourning or crying or pain." (You won't even mind if your crazy uncle is there.) For this reason, sin cannot exist there. "Nothing impure will ever enter it, nor will anyone who does what is shameful or deceitful."[34] If sin separates us from God, then it cannot exist in a place where we will see God face to face. So there will be no sinning in heaven. But I guarantee you, it won't be missed. In heaven, the ones we've lost are perfectly happy and we will be also when we get there.

Discussion Questions

1. *How have you viewed heaven in the past—as a place of excitement or as one of boredom?*

2. *What's the first question you'd like to ask God when you get to heaven?*

3. *What did you learn about hell from this chapter?*

4. *How do the concepts of heaven and hell motivate you to share your faith with others?*

5. *What is the greatest thing about heaven to you?*

---

34 *Revelation 21:4, 27, NIV.*

CON
CLU
SION//

✳ ✳ ✳ The great Christian apologist and writer G. K. Chesterton once said about the Christian faith, "I did not make it. . . . It made me."[1]

The truths we've explored in this book are the bedrock of historic Christianity. We're not responsible to shape them, but we are shaped and formed by them. These truths require attention, focus, and time. As we learn them, we find our faith more exhilarating. We worship God with greater passion and commitment. We live with firmer conviction and grace toward others. The more we understand God's uncensored truth, the more amazing his uncensored grace appears.

Dorothy Sayers brilliantly and memorably noted the excitement that comes from knowing God's truth:

> Official Christianity, of late years, has been having what is known as a bad press. We are constantly assured that the churches are empty because preachers insist too much upon doctrine—dull dogma as people call it. The fact is the precise opposite. It is the neglect of dogma that makes for dullness. The Christian faith is the most exciting drama that ever staggered the imagination of man—and the dogma is the drama. . . . Now, we may call that doctrine exhilarating, or we may call it devastating; we may call it revelation, or we may call it rubbish; but if we call it dull, then words have no meaning at all.[2]

---

1   G. K. Chesterton, Orthodoxy, in The Collected Works of G. K. Chesterton *(Fort Collins, CO: Ignatius Press, 1986), 211.*

2   *Dorothy Sayers,* Creed or Chaos? *(New York: Harcort, Brace, 1949), 25.*

As we've seen in the following pages, God's truth is any-thing but dull. It challenges our assumptions, corrects our perspectives, and focuses us on the God who created all things for his own glory. Truth grounds us, keeping us from sliding into what the Bible warns about in Jude 3-4: "Defend the faith that God has entrusted once for all time to his holy people. I say this because some ungodly people have wormed their way into your churches, saying that God's marvelous grace allows us to live immoral lives. The condemnation of such people was recorded long ago, for they have denied our only Master and Lord, Jesus Christ."

We have received this uncensored grace, but it is not a license to live immorally. It is an opportunity to be transformed. It's okay to not be okay, but we don't have to stay that way! We need both uncensored grace and uncensored truth. And by growing in his truth, we'll emulate Jesus, who came as one full of both grace and truth. May truth shape us each day of our lives as we grow in our faith and life.

✳ ✳ ✳ I am so thankful for the many faithful men and women who have gone before me, who have helped me understand the Christian faith. They are too many to name, but their teaching, writing, and influence have made all the difference.

To Roy Wheeler for showing me that life and ministry are about loving people and that truth must live in service to people. Thanks for being the first (and for a while the only) person who believed God could use me as a pastor!

To Keith Ray for grabbing me as a freshman in college, sticking Stanley Jaki's *The Relevance of Physics* in my hand, and challenging me to think about all of life from a Christian perspective.

To Mike Bodine and the entire staff of Central Christian Church. 1-2-3, you rock!

To David Stroder for your research that laid the framework for this book years ago.

To Jared Wilson of Docent Research Group for your awesomeness and your help in pulling this manuscript together in a much clearer, more developed form.

To Mary Wilhite for living the faith for eighty years and filling our home with books that pointed me to God. I can't believe I'm writing this, but I miss getting all the clippings and quotes you sent me during your life! Thanks for showing me that faith is alive in the small acts of kindness and trust we exhibit every day.

To Lori Wilhite, my beautiful bride, for loving me through it all and for your constant encouragement and support. I love doing life with you!

To Emma and Ethan for teaching me so much about God and myself. I pray these truths sustain you throughout your lives.

✳ ✳ ✳ **Jud Wilhite is senior pastor of Central Christian Church.** Thousands attend Central's campuses along with a global community who attend online. Jud is the author of several books, including *Eyes Wide Open* and *Uncensored Grace*. Under Jud's leadership, Central is dedicated to helping people find their way to God. He is known for his conversational approach to teaching the Bible and his passion to help others know God and love him more. Jud and his wife, Lori, reside in the Las Vegas area with their two children and a slobbery Bulldog named Roxy.